Introducing ... Coluzzle

A "must" tool for the beginning to expert scrapbooker!

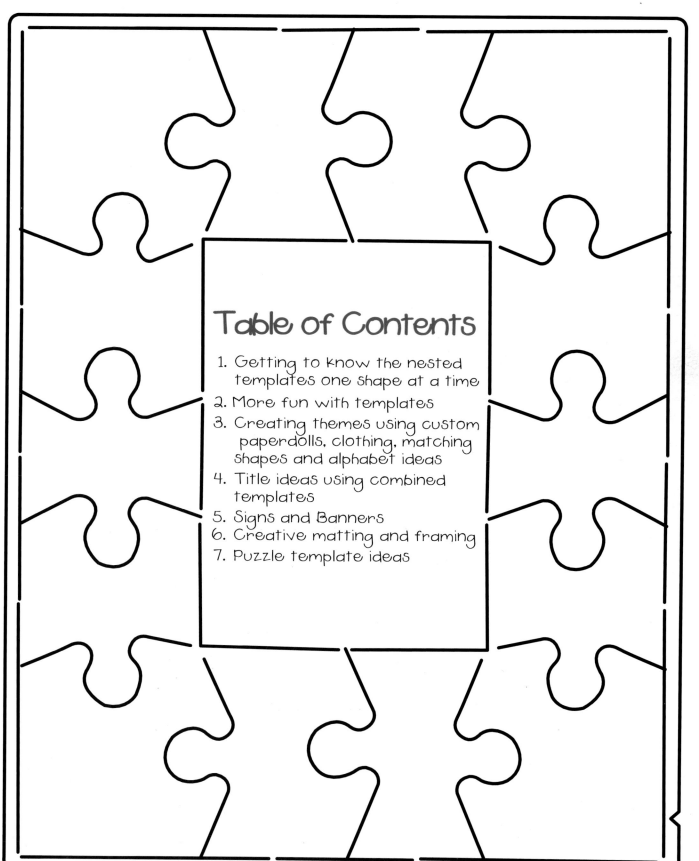

Table of Contents

The Basics

Complete instructions are included with Coluzzle® products. The following information will help you understand the cutting system in more detail.

Coluzzle® Templates
- All Coluzzle® Brand Templates are made using a laser to cut each channel. The width of the channel is controlled so that the Guarded™ Swivel Knife will fit down into the channel to cut perfect shapes time and time again.
- Remove the adhesive coating that covers both sides of every template before using.
- Handle templates with care and avoid dropping.
- Templates can be stored vertically or horizontally. Never place objects under or on top of your templates.
- Always store templates away from excessive heat or cold temperatures.

Guarded™ Swivel Knife
- Insert the swivel knife blade into the channel of the template with the guard facing the direction you are cutting.
- Always hold the swivel knife straight up and down. Never tilt the knife handle from side to side or front to back.
- With firm pressure, push down on the swivel knife and pierce the surface you are cutting with the tip of the blade. The action of pulling the blade without moving your fingers or wrist and applying consistent downward pressure while you pull the swivel knife is the secret to success.
- Never force your swivel knife.
- When blades become dull, always replace with a Coluzzle® Guarded™ Swivel Blade.

Easy Glide™ Cutting Mat
- Never use anything but the Guarded™ Swivel Knife on your Easy Glide™ Cutting Mat.
- Apply the chipboard provided on a standard 8-1/2 x 11 paper pad to back your cutting mat. This will stiffen the cutting mat and allow you to turn it over and make straight cuts with a craft knife without damaging the cutting surface of your Easy Glide™ Cutting Mat.
- The Easy Glide™ Cutting Mat does not have a memory and will not bounce back, so do not set anything on it that might cause it to dent or to be crushed.

Web
- "Webs" keep the template together so that the template does not fall into a bunch of pieces! **Never break apart the templates.**
- Not only do webs keep templates together, but they serve as a start and stopping point when cutting. Always start a cut at the beginning of a web and jump over a web to continue cutting.

Notch
- The border of some puzzle templates have a tiny notch, which serves as an orientation point. Make sure to keep the notch in the same position throughout your project. If a notch is not provided in your template, make sure your template is oriented the same way throughout your project.

Cutting
- When working, remember the blade steers itself, so don't move your fingers or wrist. It's just a simple pull of the arm! (Think of shifting gears in a car – it's the same movement!)
- Make sure the image you are cutting is totally inside your template channels.

The Coluzzle® Templates

4.875 x 4.875
Circle

5.25 x 6.625
Elongated
Oval

6 x 5.5
Hexagon

4.25 x 5
Paper Doll

5 x 7
Rectangle Puzzle

4.625 x 5.375
Oval

6 x 4.875
Heart

9.125 x 8.25
Heart Puzzle

8.625 x 10.625
Large Rectangle Puzzle

5.5 x 5.5
Square

6 x 6.25
Star

11.75 x 11.75
Large Square Puzzle

Coming soon....
Even more
Coluzzle®
shapes to
choose and
create from!!!

5.25 x 6.5
Rectangle

8.25 x 10.625
Oval Puzzle

8.125 x 10
Bear Puzzle

8.5 x 8.25
Star Puzzle

11.625 x 14.75
Extra Large Rectangle Puzzle

ABCDE
FGHIJ
KLMN)
OPQRS
TUVW
XYZ!.?

8.5 x 11
Alphabet

Due to manufacturing processes, templates may not precisely match patterns.

5

Terms we use...

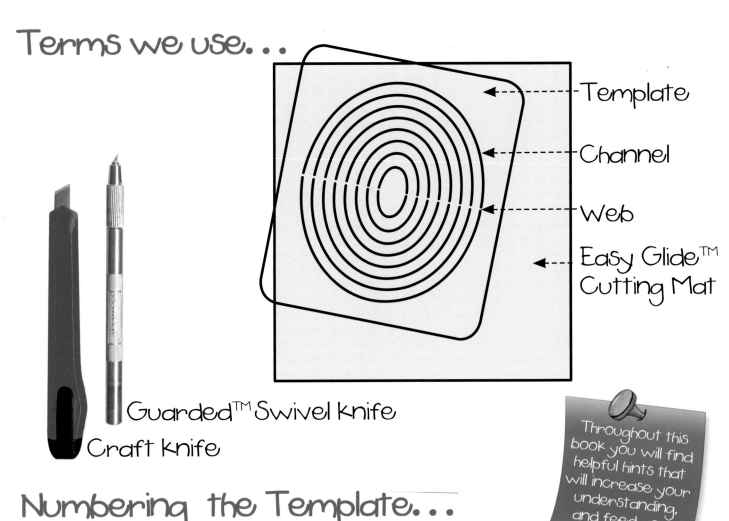

Template

Channel

Web

Easy Glide™ Cutting Mat

Guarded™ Swivel Knife

Craft Knife

Throughout this book you will find helpful hints that will increase your understanding, and feed your creativity.

Numbering the Template...

We highly suggest numbering the channels on each of your templates from the outside in. We have referred to each channel by number throughout the book. Try drawing each number with a permanent marker on the underside of the template. If you prefer, color coding beside each number can be helpful.

Remember to be patient ... some of our greatest designs began with mistakes!

To make cutting your photos a little clearer, use a plain sheet of cardstock to cut out each size of one shape. Mark each cut with the corresponding channel number. Then use these cuts to determine which size works best for you.

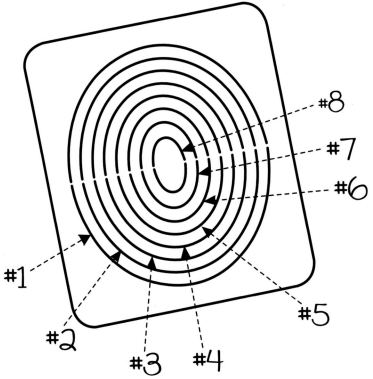

#8

#7

#6

#1

#2

#3

#4

#5

6

Anatomy 101
Coluzzle® Paper Doll Template

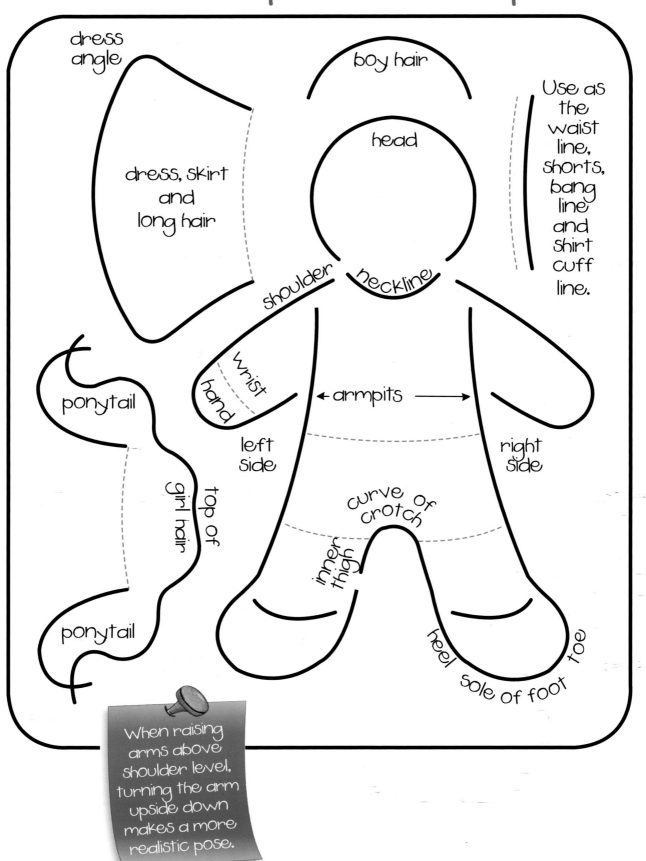

dress angle

boy hair

head

dress, skirt and long hair

Use as the waist line, shorts, bang line and shirt cuff line.

shoulder

neckline

wrist

hand

armpits

ponytail

top of girl hair

left side

right side

curve of crotch

inner thigh

ponytail

heel

sole of foot

toe

When raising arms above shoulder level, turning the arm upside down makes a more realistic pose.

"Cheating"

While the nested Coluzzle® templates offer a great variety of shapes to work with, they have an almost unlimited creative potential with a trick that we call "cheating." There are several ways that each of the templates can be cheated.

Method 1: Cheating for a smaller size

The first method simply makes the cutout smaller than the original channel. This is by far the most common method used in this book.

Give it a try . . .

Using the template and a sheet of white cardstock, cut one half of one channel, web to web (shown in red). Instead of completing the second half of the square, slide the template to the right so that the channel is lined up with the first cut. Now make the second cut in the channel of the square, beginning just before the corner (shown in blue). Congratulations! You have just cheated the template! This method is very useful with the square, heart, rectangle and hexagon, but can be used with any of the shapes. By adjusting the length of the slide, you can make your cut as wide or as narrow as you like. You can combine a vertical and a horizontal slide to produce an almost endless combination of cuts.

Method 1

1st cut red   2nd cut blue

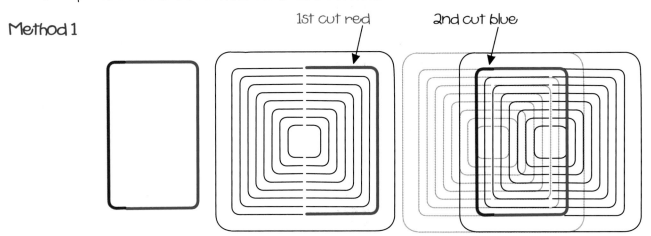

Method 2: Cheating for a larger size . . . sometimes referred to as lengthening.

This method is very similar to the first and is very useful with the paper doll and straight-sided nested templates.

Give it a try . . .

Using the template and white cardstock, make the first cut (shown in red). Now slide the template to desired size and make the second cut (shown in blue). Wahoo, you have successfully cheated for a larger shape! Both Method 1 and Method 2 require a little practice, but once you get going, we know that you will find yourself "cheating" on everything!

Method 2

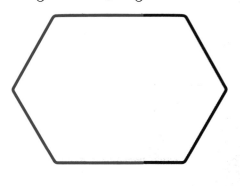
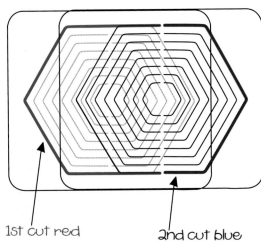

1st cut red   2nd cut blue

Method 3: Pivoting

This method began with the circle, but now we use it with any shape! Let your imagination be your guide!

Give it a try ...

Using the circle template and a white (it's easier to see the cuts on white) sheet of cardstock, cut approximately 1/3 of the circle (shown in red). Without lifting the template, pivot one end up or down, making sure that the channel you want to use for your second cut crosses the previous cut at some point. Now make the second cut (shown in blue). Using straight edge scissors, cut the open end of the shape. You've done it! These cuts can be very narrow or wide. Remember, the channel you use for the second cut of the pivot does not have to be the same as the first. Experiment!

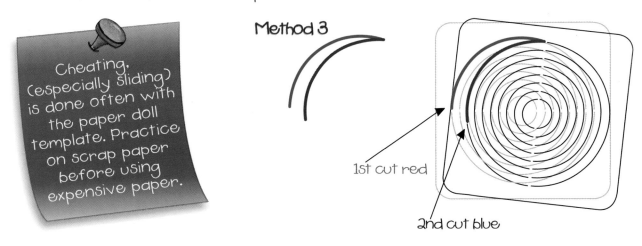

Cheating, (especially sliding) is done often with the paper doll template. Practice on scrap paper before using expensive paper.

Method 3

1st cut red

2nd cut blue

Method 4: Sliding

This method allows you to customize any shape to your needs.

Give it a try ...

Begin any cut. **While keeping the knife in the channel,** slide and or curve the template to desired position. The knife will follow along while cutting or sliding for a perfect custom design. You can slide **any** template!

Method 4

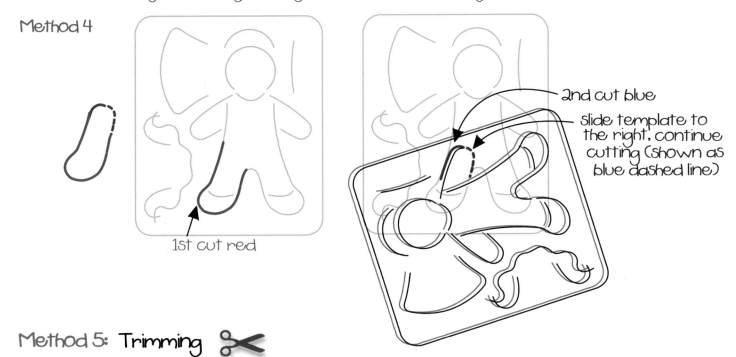

1st cut red

2nd cut blue

slide template to the right, continue cutting (shown as blue dashed line)

Method 5: Trimming ✂

Some shapes are impossible to make using only the templates. By trimming with scissors any shape can be created. Occasionally trimming is used to connect one template shape to another. Scissors are necessary to cut out several articles of custom paper doll clothing.

Getting To Know Each Template...
Using what you've learned, lets create some simple shapes using only one template.

An easy to follow template guide can be found at the top of each page. This will allow you to have all of your templates handy before beginning your project.

Using Only The
Heart

Ornament
The bottom of the #5 heart, trimmed with decorative and "Big cut" scissors

Butterfly
upper wing
#5 heart

lower wing
#6 heart

#6 cheated heart

apple leaf

body - #5 heart

strawberries
#6 & #7 heart
trim green hearts for stems

Apple
#3 heart

trim with #6 heart
↓

Using Only The
Circle

Candy
#8 circle x2 - cut one circle in half with decorative scissors

Glasses
#7 & #8 circle

nose piece
#7 & #8 oval

#8 & #9 elongated oval

Pocket Watch
#7 heart center cut out by hand

rim - #4 circle
face - #5 circle
center hole punch

Citrus
#4 circle (white portion is slightly trimmed on the straight edge)

Happy Face
#1 circle

smile - #6 & #7 oval trimmed

eyes - #9 elongated oval

When cutting one nested shape inside another (i.e., Olympic rings), cut the inside shape first to help prevent the shape from slipping on the second cut.

Olympic Rings
#6 & #7 circles intertwined

Clock
face - #1 & #2 circle
base - #1 & #6 heart bottom
hands - #1 rectangle (cheated inward)
numbers - "Fat Dot" Alphabitties

Window

outside –
#7 square
inside –
#6 square

Kite

trim here for pink & blue

trim here for yellow & green

kite
sections

#7 cheated
square
(trim dotted
lines by hand)

kite bows

To brush up on
"cheating" turn
to page 8 & 9
for complete
instructions.

Candy
#6 cheated square
Wrapping – the corner
of any square (trim with
decorative scissors)

horizontal kite frame

vertical kite frame

Gone
Fishin'

Lemonade

Lemonade stand

all – #4 cheated
square

Cactus
arms – #1–#3 square
body – any square

Gone Fishin'
#7 cheated square
sign post –
#1–#3 square

10¢

Using Only The
Elongated Oval

Menorrah

#1 - #8 elongated oval, turn template sideways and cut on every channel leaving a small portion in center uncut.

base
#7 elongated oval

Beehive - #2-7 elongated oval opening is #8 elongated oval

flame is 1/2 of heart punch candle cups are 1/2 of oval punch

UFO

Canoe

#3 elongated oval

←canoe sides - #1 elongated oval

water - cut with "wave" deep cut scissors

#7 & #8 elongated ovals

#9 elongated oval

Alien

UFO

Using Only The
Rectangle

Firecracker

#4 cheated rectangle
star punches

Popsicle

top - #8 hexagon
bottom - #5 cheated
   rectangle
sticks - #6 cheated
   rectangle

Digital Clock

face - #1 cheated rectangle
number sections - #7 cheated
   rectangle (cheated by cutting
   left side, sliding template left, then
   cutting right side)

Toothbrush

bristles - #7 cheated
   rectangle
handle - #1 rectangle

speaker

legs and antenna -
any rectangle

Television

body - #2 rectangle
screen - #4 rectangle

Using Only The
Hexagon

Hockey Stick
#1 hexagon slightly pivoted outward at outer end of stick

Pocket
hexagon/square hankie - star points

The channels of the square and hexagon templates fit together perfectly on each size. Use them to create shapes such as the denim pocket and the gift tag. (page 66).

Hockey Puck
#1 oval

Purse
#3 hexagon
flap - #6 hexagon

purse handle
#6 & #7 oval

circle punch

lengthened hexagon
(see method 4, page 9 for lengthening instructions)

← square →

Convertible -
top - #1-#2 hexagon
body - #2 cheated rectangle
grill - #8 rectangle
lights - #8 square
antenna - #1 oval

Soccer Goal
pictured on page 54

15

Using Only The Star

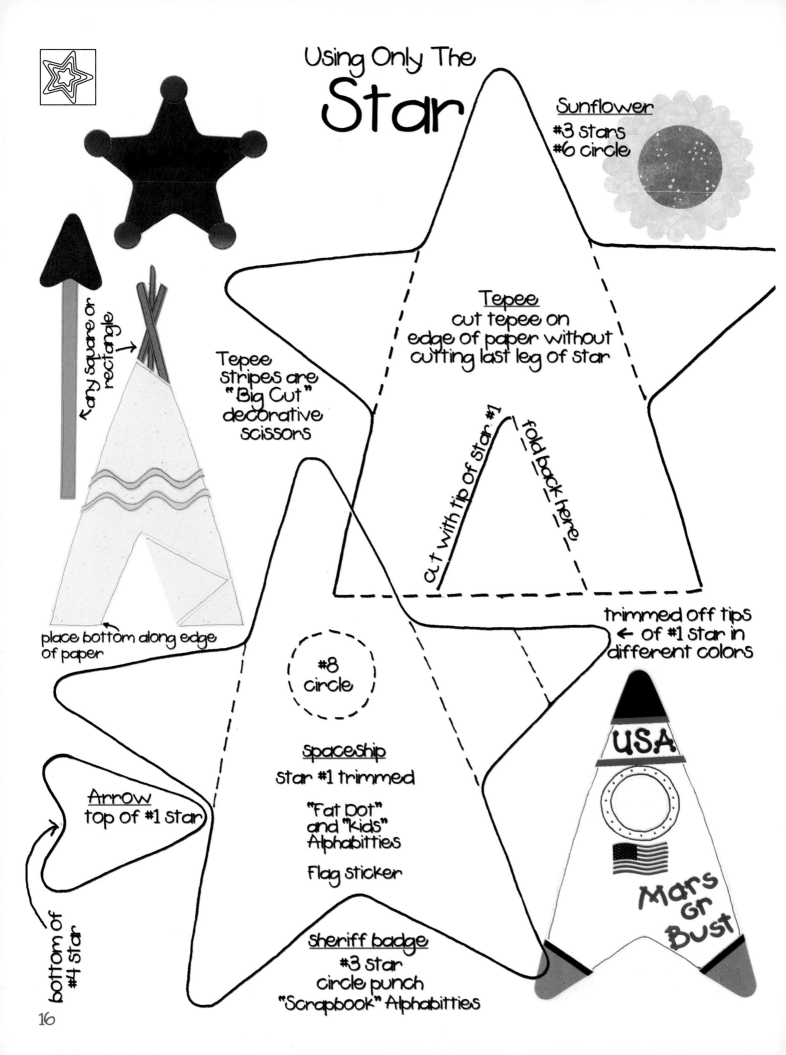

Sunflower
#3 stars
#6 circle

Tepee
cut tepee on
edge of paper without
cutting last leg of star

Tepee
stripes are
"Big Cut"
decorative
scissors

← any square or rectangle

place bottom along edge of paper

cut with tip of star #1

fold back here

trimmed off tips
← of #1 star in
different colors

#8
circle

Spaceship
star #1 trimmed

"Fat Dot"
and "Kids"
Alphabitties

Flag sticker

USA

Mars
Gr
Bust

Arrow
top of #1 star

bottom of #4 star

Sheriff badge
#3 star
circle punch
"Scrapbook" Alphabitties

16

Using Only The
Oval

Rainbow
#1-7 oval

Pinecone
leaves - #3 oval (trimmed)
pieces - #8 oval
body - #3 oval
tip - #7 oval

Bow
center - #8 oval
bow - #7 oval
ties - #3-#4 scooted oval

Baby Face - #5 oval
bow - 2 #8 ovals
bow center - circle punch
headband - #5 cheated oval

Bananas
#3 cheated oval

Watermelon
green - #1-#2 oval
white #2-#3 oval
red #3 oval cut in half

Chain
#7-#8 oval interlocked

Using The Paper Doll Template ...

Some items, (often custom clothing) that appear throughout this book are not made with templates. The "scissor" ✂ symbol will show you where a full size custom pattern has been added for your convenience.

All of the clothing on this page has been made using only the paper doll template, (✂ unless otherwise noted).

The pants and shorts are slightly cheated inward toward each inner thigh.

top ✂

Basket - hexagon

sandals x2 - cheat bottom of foot, leaving space for strap.

hand trim sides of strap

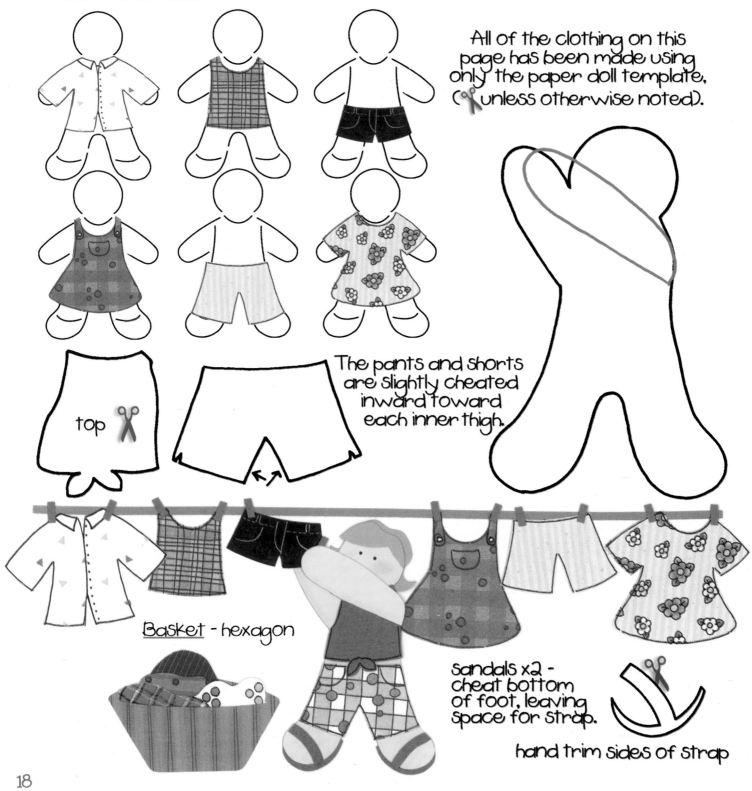

Paper Doll Positioning

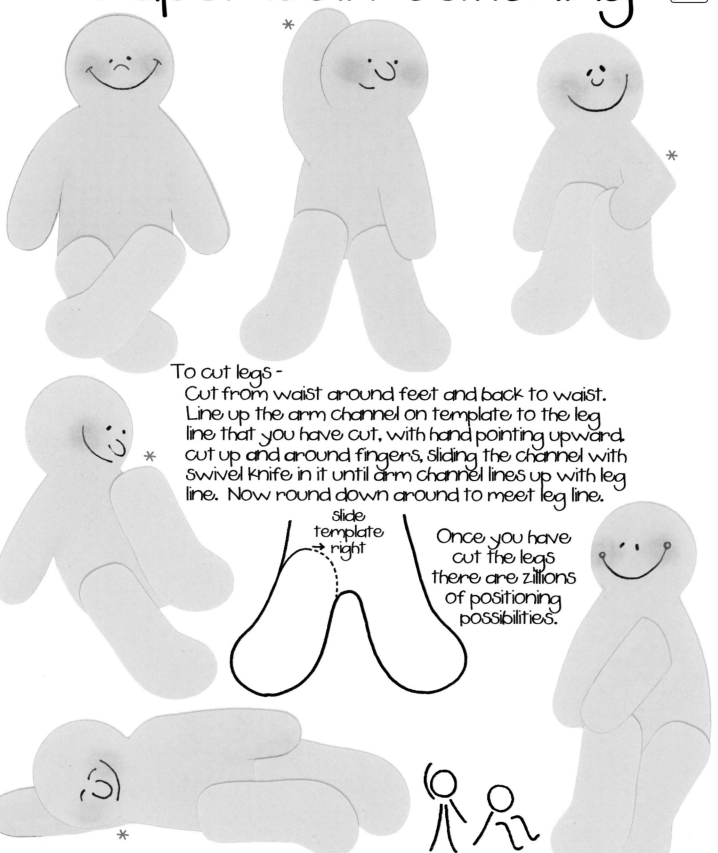

To cut legs -
Cut from waist around feet and back to waist.
Line up the arm channel on template to the leg
line that you have cut, with hand pointing upward.
Cut up and around fingers, sliding the channel with
swivel knife in it until arm channel lines up with leg
line. Now round down around to meet leg line.

slide
template
→ right

Once you have
cut the legs
there are zillions
of positioning
possibilities.

* To position arms or legs, draw a stick figure first on scratch paper. Cut around
head first. Position template around, (using the sliding method page 9, method 4).
Cut each limb separately. It's a lot easier than it sounds.

19

Paper Doll Sizing

By "sliding" to lengthen the sides, legs and arms of the doll template, you can make **any** size doll.

*from dad to toddler ... all from one easy to use template

*momma

teen or * big kid

*kid

*toddler

*cheat inward

Sun Glasses

use the curve of the crotch to make the frames then color the lens black and add sides

cut out shoes, leave this heel portion un-cut, then cut spikey or chunky high heels

Tiny Infant - Cut foot and leg until you run into end of leg, keep knife in the channel upward. Cut head, then trim down or use a large circle punch.

sandals x2 use foot template

cut around foot then clip out strap area

mary jane x2

top of dress *

Skirt *

Toddler Boy (opposite page)

arm *

body and right leg *

left leg *

sitting baby *

T-Shirt cheat outward

little girl jumper *

trim off

#8 oval cheated down

brim *

hat top top of head

cut solid sections then cheat dotted sections toward center of doll

small star punch

hand drawn

arms and legs x4

bear body

bear head

ear x2

Bear

body - #8 circle trim with decorative scissors

21

Paper Doll Expressions

Happy

The Micron .01 tip is perfect for lining faces

Laughing

Sleepy

Circle hole punches work well for eyes, cheeks and noses

Glasses and Goggles

Cheeks - apply pink chalk with a Q-Tip or eye shadow applicator

*If you don't find the expression you're looking for, try looking in the comics or children's storybooks.

22

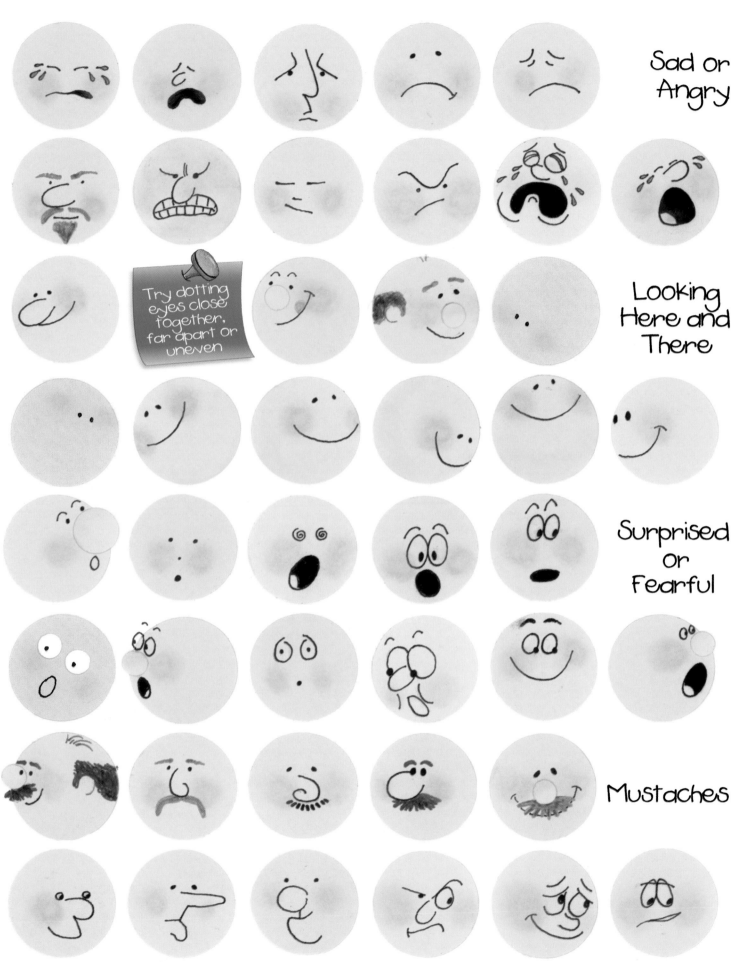

Sad or Angry

Try dotting eyes close together, far apart or uneven

Looking Here and There

Surprised or Fearful

Mustaches

*For even more expression ideas look on pages 24 and 25.

23

Paper Doll Hair

From these ...

To ... any hairstyle imaginable!

Try connecting the top of girl or boy hair to the skirt for a "long hair, behind the ears" look

clip into bangs with straight edge scissors

angle any curve toward part

mini scallop scissors

waistline bangs (insert head under bangs)

curve of crotch

bangs - any cheated oval curve of crotch

girl hair with girl hair bangs

waistline curve

2 pony-tails

#7 oval →

girl hair with boy hair bangs

mini scallop scissors

cheat inward on head or circle

leg and → top of foot

oval →

24

hand shape around hair and bangs for a wavy look

#7 lengthened circle, then trim bottom with waistline headband - boy hair cheated downward

top - #6 heart

inside - #7 upside down heart (place head behind bangs)
Place heel of foot of doll on dots and continue cutting up inside of leg and around curve of crotch to make flip.
Trim bottom by hand.

headband - cheated head
bow - 2 wings of a butterfly sticker attached at center

#6 oval →

#7 circle cut 2/3 for top 1/3 for bangs (trim)

hair - #7 circle
bangs - #6 circle
barrettes - try oval, rectangle, star, heart or diamond punches (small stickers also make great barrettes)

hair - girl hair top, skirt bottom
bangs - #7 heart top

← cheated boy hair

#7 cheated heart

#7 cheated hearts

pivoted girl hair

upside down boy hair (cut top straight, clip)

girl hair turned upside down

clipping

notches

notches

lots of notches

any curve makes side part

add handcut cowlick

25

Now That You've Learned To

use each template alone, let's combine
several templates and get really creative!

<u>House</u> - #5 rectangle
   door - #5 cheated rectangle
   roof - #2 hexagon (top 1/3)

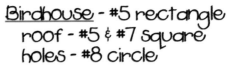

<u>Birdhouse</u> - #5 rectangle
   roof - #5 & #7 square
   holes - #8 circle

<u>Picket
Fence</u>

#3 - #4
Square

1. Mark cardstock to desired height of fence. Mark a second line 1/4" below the first line.
2. Line up template with edge of page. Cut #1, #2, #3 and #4 channels under the second marked line. Move template to the left, placing the #1 channel on top of the fourth line cut. Continue cutting the #2, #3 and #4 channels until you've reached your desired length. Leave bottoms of pickets attached to one another.
3. Lengthen channels #1 and #2 to adhere horizontally to your pickets. Let glue dry completely, then trim top and bottom, using your top marked line to guide the trimming of the picket points.

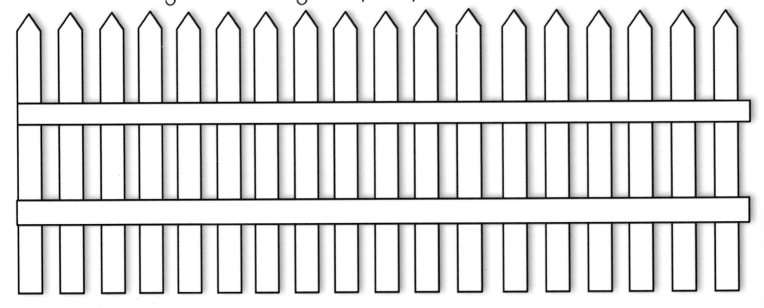

Combining Templates...

let the fun begin!

Fries -
container -
#5 square
fries -
any square
or rectangle

Burger -
bun #4 circle
tomato - #6 circle
cheese - #5 square

Use the Coluzzle® nested templates to cut out paper piecing patterns. Instead of tracing the basic shapes like circles or ovals, use the template closest to the size your pattern calls for, then trim if necessary.

Cup - cheated rectangle
sign - #6 circle

Joe's Drive-In

Mug - #5 square and
#1 elongated oval
handle - #6 & #7 oval
steam punch

Taco - #1 oval
tomato - #5 circle
lettuce - trim with "deckle"
decorative scissors

Tea kettle -
kettle - #2 circle
spout - #8 square
lid top - small circle punch

lid - #5 circle
handle #1 circle

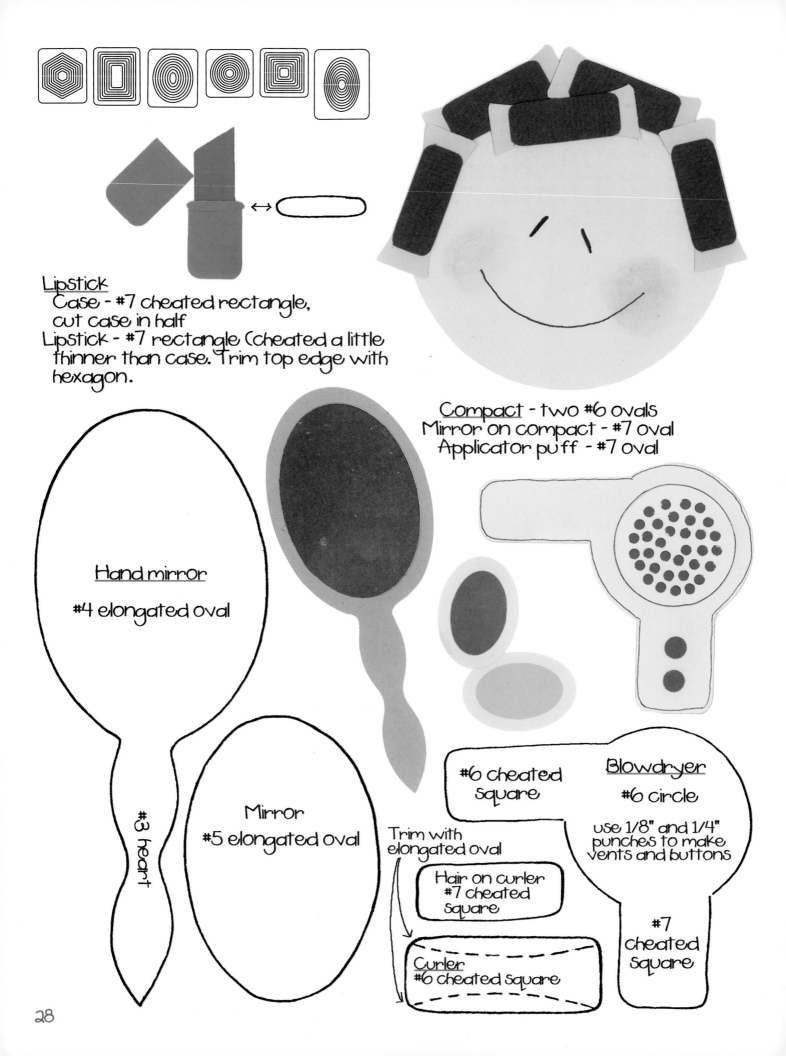

Lipstick
Case - #7 cheated rectangle,
cut case in half
Lipstick - #7 rectangle (cheated a little
thinner than case. Trim top edge with
hexagon.

Compact - two #6 ovals
Mirror on compact - #7 oval
Applicator puff - #7 oval

Hand mirror
#4 elongated oval

#3 heart

Mirror
#5 elongated oval

Trim with
elongated oval

#6 cheated
square

Hair on curler
#7 cheated
square

Curler
#6 cheated square

Blowdryer
#6 circle

use 1/8" and 1/4"
punches to make
vents and buttons

#7
cheated
square

28

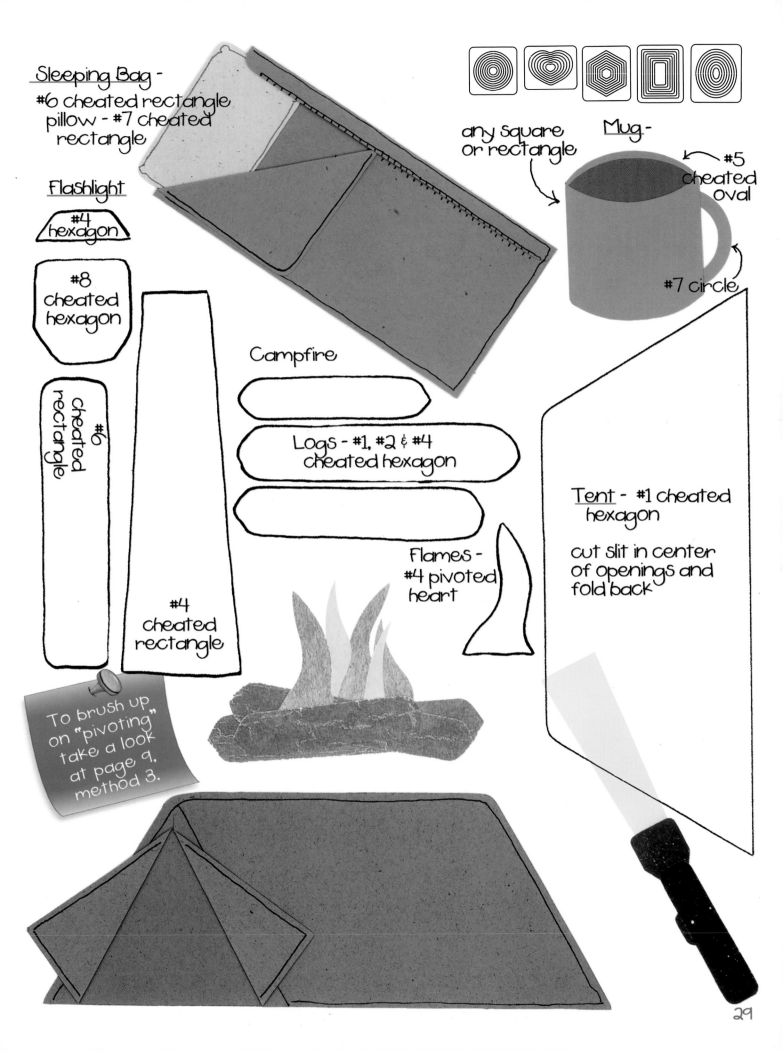

Sleeping Bag -
#6 cheated rectangle
pillow - #7 cheated
rectangle

Flashlight

#4 hexagon

#8 cheated hexagon

#6 cheated rectangle

#4 cheated rectangle

any square or rectangle

Mug -

#5 cheated oval

#7 circle

Campfire

Logs - #1, #2 & #4 cheated hexagon

Flames - #4 pivoted heart

Tent - #1 cheated hexagon

cut slit in center of openings and fold back

To brush up on "pivoting" take a look at page 9, method 3.

29

teddy & cat nose

tail

cat ear

Paw Print
#4 heart
#8 circle

Cat
head - #5 oval
body - #3 circle
hands - #8 circle
feet - #7 oval
tummy - #5 circle

Caged Monkey
cage - #1 cheated square
muzzle - #5 oval
ears - #7 circle
head - #6 oval
body - #1 circle

Teddy
head - #5 oval
body - #3 circle
hands - #8 circle
feet - #7 oval
tummy - #5 circle
ears - #8 circle
inside ears - large circle
    hole punch
eyes - circle punch

chick beak

Chick or Duck
head - #5 oval
body - #3 circle
feet - bottom of
    #6 heart (round
    out top of
    feet with
    #8 circle
wings - #7
    cheated
    oval
tail -#1 &
    #2 circle

30

Use the hexagon pattern for the sun (see page 37) to help you position ovals and circles for these flowers.

Pink Flower
#8 oval
#8 circle

Coneflower
petals - #8 oval
stem - #1 oval

Bee
body - #8
  elongated oval
wings - #7 heart

Posey - Cut 1/2 of
  #7 circles and go
  to next petal
center - #7 circle
petals - #4 circle

Daisy
stem - #1 & #2 heart
leaf & petals - #6
  cheated heart
center - #8 circle

stem

daisy
leaf

Sunflower
petals - #7 oval
center - #7 circle
leaves - #1 cheated
  elongated oval

Now That You're An Expert...
let's create some original themes.

Boy

1. #8 circle (cut off both legs at upper thigh)
2. Slide the toe to round off the "knee" of one leg. (see page 9, method 4)
3. Cut off hands and trim with scallop scissors, place one on coconut and one on tree.

<u>Palm Tree</u>

Trunk - #1 oval

Coconuts - circle punch

Fronds - #1 or #2 circles cut in half (take notches off with straight scissors)

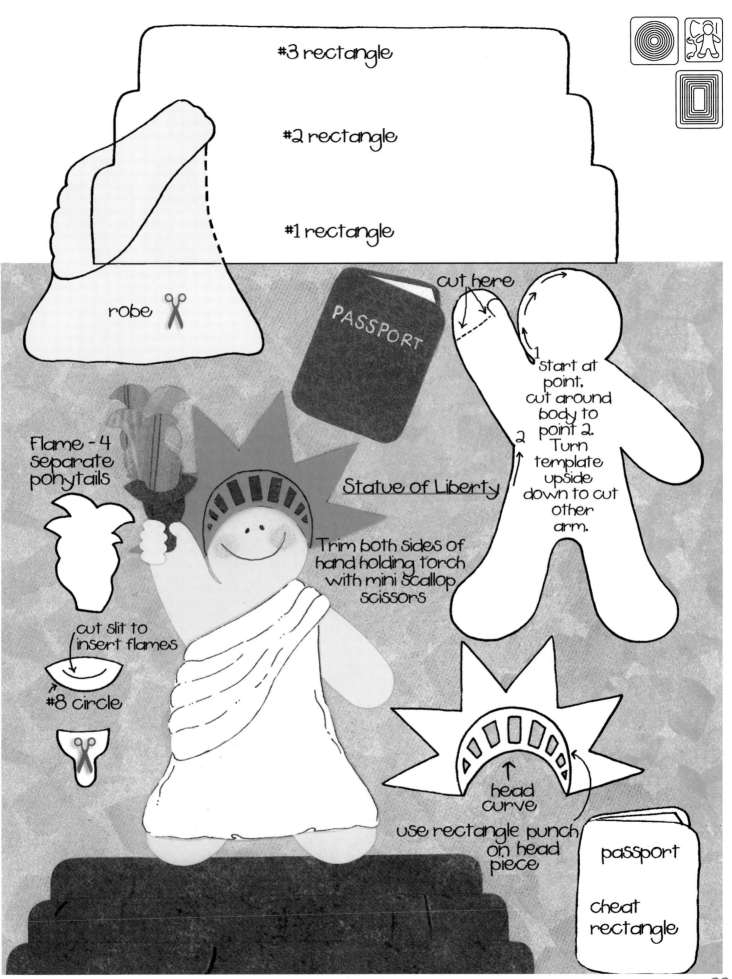

#3 rectangle

#2 rectangle

#1 rectangle

robe ✂

PASSPORT

cut here

1
2

Start at point, cut around body to point 2. Turn template upside down to cut other arm.

Flame - 4 separate ponytails

Statue of Liberty

Trim both sides of hand holding torch with mini scallop scissors

cut slit to insert flames

#8 circle

head curve

use rectangle punch on head piece

passport

cheat rectangle

33

ROAD TRIP

ONE WAY

MAP

sun screen

One Way Sign
background - #1 cheated rectangle
point - #2 cheated star (connect
  tip to shaft with points of any star)
arrow shaft - any cheated rectangle

hat

← top of
  head

← #7
  oval

Bermudas

cheat

socks

outline
of
foot

hair

If patterned paper
makes cutting two-
step cuts (like
cheating), difficult,
make the first cut
on the front
(pattern) side of
paper, then turn over
and make the second
cut on the back.

shirt

← #7 rectangle
  fold on
  dotted lines

map

basket
handle

#8
cheated
square

sandal
bottom

sandal
strip

outline
of
foot

top of
girl hair

bangs

Basket

#7 cheated rectangle

right
side
of
basket

tuck
behind
head

capri
pants

cheat

sun
screen

#8 cheated
square

towel

haltertop

glasses

Suitcase
#7 & #8 hexagon
#5 rectangle

bottoms of flip-flops
are the outline of feet

large and small
flower punch

Camera - #5 cheated rectangle
  lens - #7 & #8 circles (use a circle
    punch on inside of #8 circle)
  handle - #8 square

Road Trip - use rectanglae punch to
  add dotted lines to letters

use small hole punch for letters

o

35

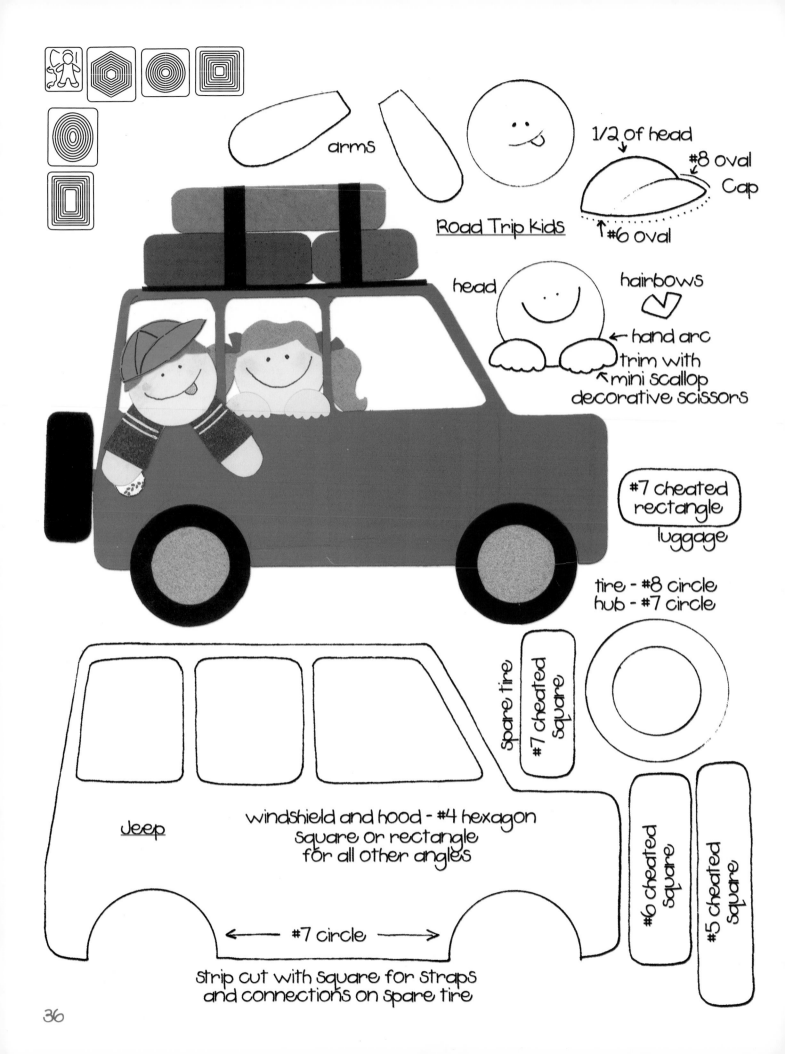

arms

Road Trip Kids

1/2 of head

#8 oval Cap

#6 oval

head

hairbows

hand arc

trim with mini scallop decorative scissors

#7 cheated rectangle

luggage

tire - #8 circle
hub - #7 circle

Spare tire

#7 cheated square

Jeep

windshield and hood - #4 hexagon
square or rectangle
for all other angles

#6 cheated square

#5 cheated square

← #7 circle →

strip cut with square for straps
and connections on spare tire

36

When making any multi-step cut (cheated shapes & combined-shape cuts) you may notice a difference in the "feel" of the knife as it slides along your first cut & then begins the second. You will find this "feel" is a great help in determining where to stop & start.

Sun

Mark points of
  #4 hexagon
Cut half of points
  of #3 star
on marked points, connect
those with shorter star
points in between.

Center - #6 circle

Try this same hexagon technique using circles and ovals to make all kinds of different flowers.

Sailboat
  base - #1 oval
  sails - #4 rectangle (trimmed diagonally)
  flag - any cheated heart
  mast - #1-#2 square

Waves
  #8 circle
  #5 oval

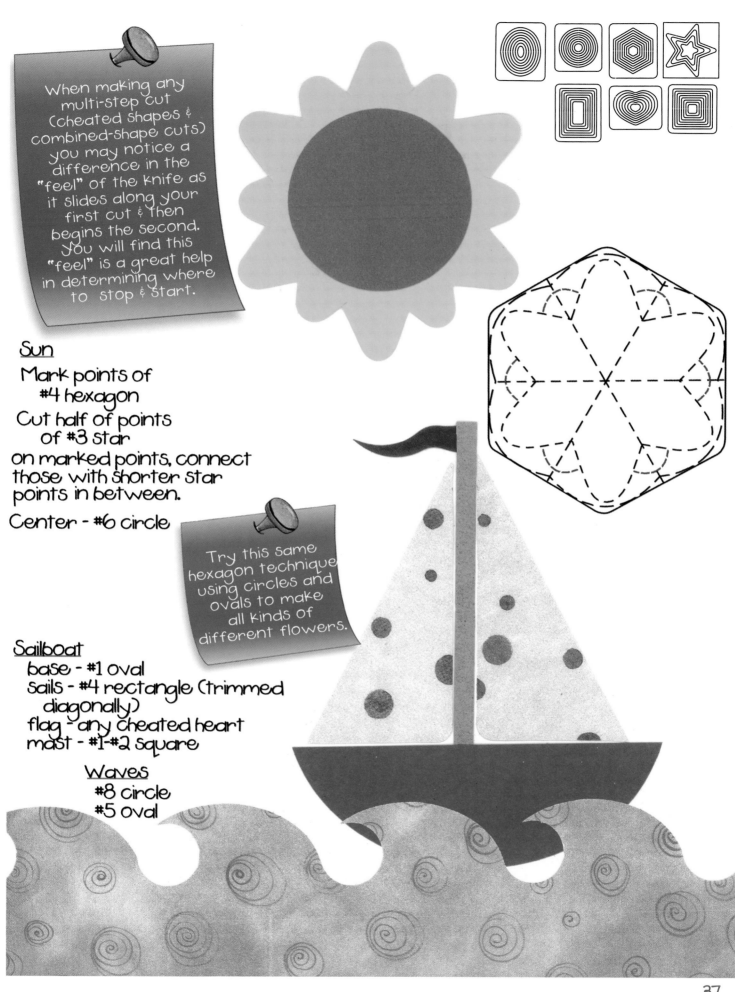

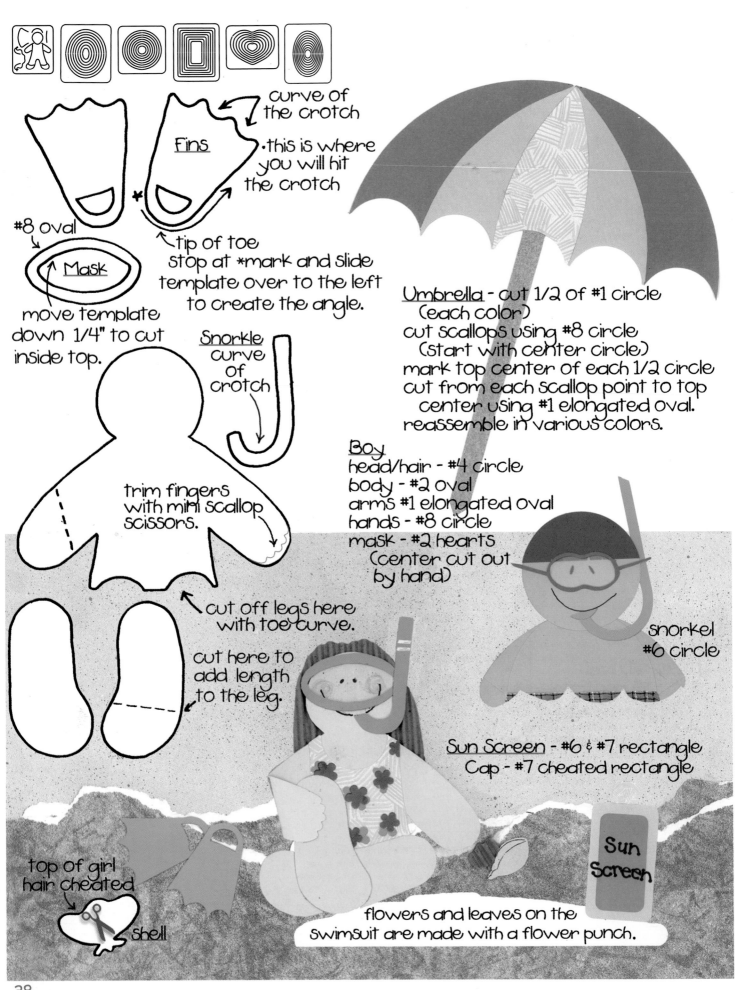

curve of
the crotch

Fins

•this is where
you will hit
the crotch

#8 oval

Mask

move template
down 1/4" to cut
inside top.

tip of toe
stop at *mark and slide
template over to the left
to create the angle.

Snorkle
curve
of
crotch

trim fingers
with mini scallop
scissors.

cut off legs here
with toe curve.

cut here to
add length
to the leg.

Umbrella - cut 1/2 of #1 circle
(each color)
cut scallops using #8 circle
(start with center circle)
mark top center of each 1/2 circle
cut from each scallop point to top
center using #1 elongated oval.
reassemble in various colors.

Boy
head/hair - #4 circle
body - #2 oval
arms #1 elongated oval
hands - #8 circle
mask - #2 hearts
(center cut out
by hand)

snorkel
#6 circle

Sun Screen - #6 & #7 rectangle
Cap - #7 cheated rectangle

top of girl
hair cheated

Shell

Sun
Screen

flowers and leaves on the
swimsuit are made with a flower punch.

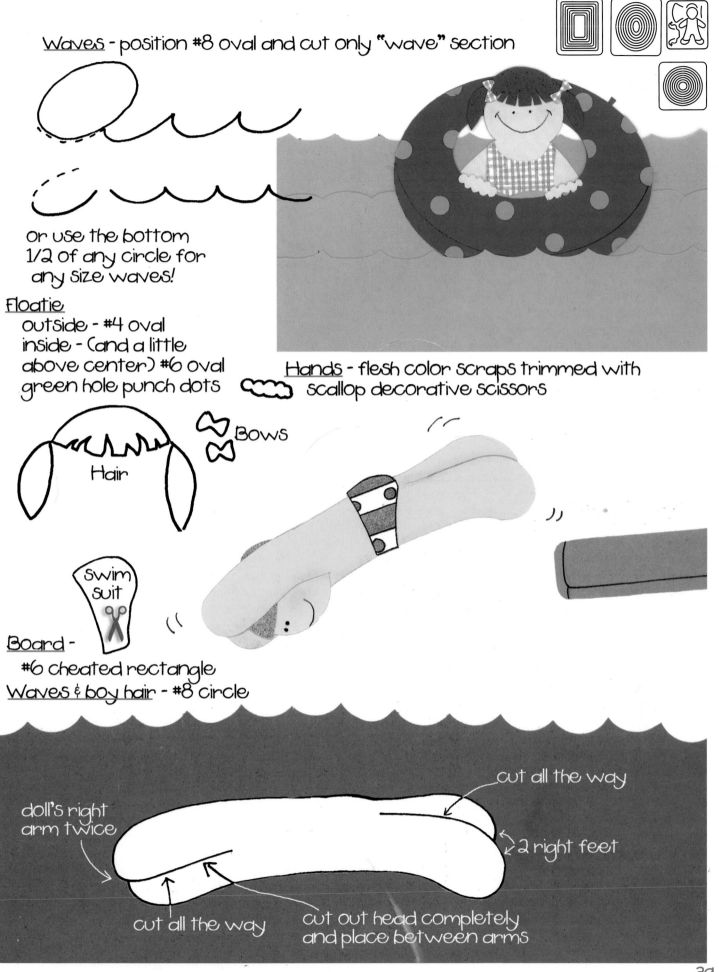

Waves - position #8 oval and cut only "wave" section

or use the bottom
1/2 of any circle for
any size waves!

Floatie
outside - #4 oval
inside - (and a little
above center) #6 oval
green hole punch dots

Hands - flesh color scraps trimmed with
scallop decorative scissors

Hair

Bows

Swim
Suit

Board -
#6 cheated rectangle
Waves & boy hair - #8 circle

cut all the way

doll's right
arm twice

2 right feet

cut all the way

cut out head completely
and place between arms

39

Ticket stub
#7 rectangle

Edges - circle punch &
"deckle" decorative scissors
"Scrapbook" alphabitties

#6 rectangle

#1 oval

top of cone

Ice Cream Cone
cone - use any rectangle

- #6 rectangle -

cone sides - twist template
toward the right and go up!
twist and repeat for left side.

Cotton
candy -
random
circles

#7 heart

#5 heart

Cone - #1 star

Corndog
#7 cheated oval
#1 rectangle

Hot dog

Ends - #8 circle
Sides - rectangle
Bun - #1 elongated oval
(cheated & trimmed)

40

WHEEEEE

any square
for lines

circle
punch
wheels

shirt #1

x3

#4 Square

#6 Oval

handle

Kid #1

Kid #2

shirt #2

Kid #3 - follow
template for
body and shirt

Seat
cheated square or
rectangle

follow doll
template
(upper
body)

circle
punch
wheels

any
square

#4 oval

#5 oval

#5 oval

lollypop

#8
circle

41

Globe - #1 circle

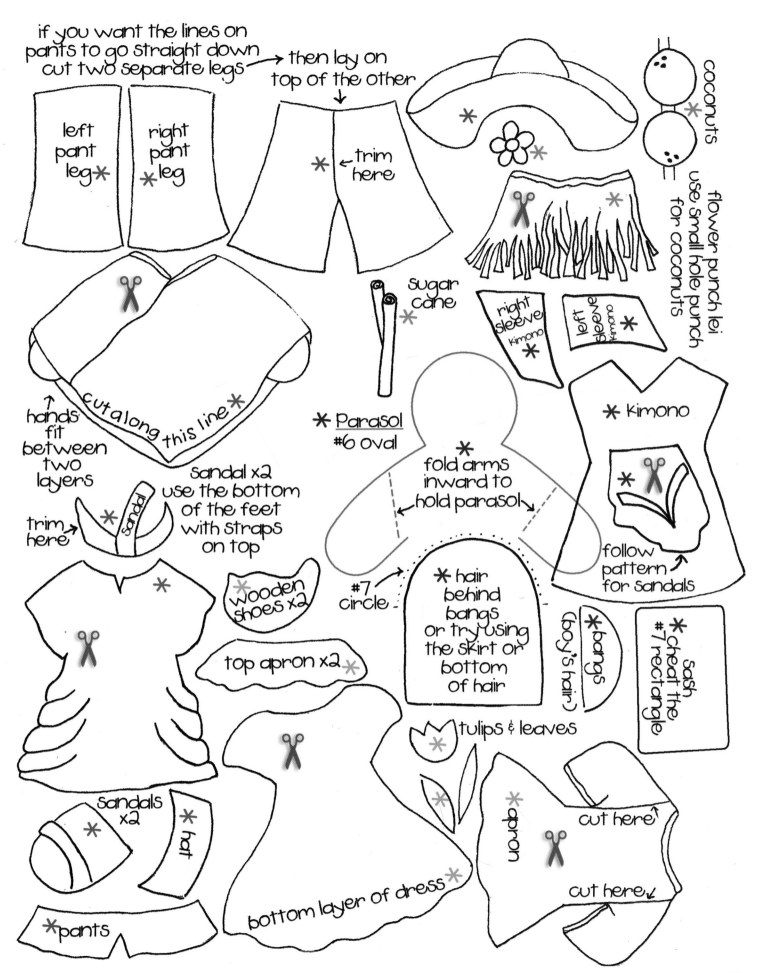

if you want the lines on pants to go straight down cut two separate legs → then lay on top of the other

left pant leg *

right pant leg *

trim here ←

* coconuts

flower punch lei use small hole punch for coconuts

* trim here ←

hands fit between two layers

cut along this line *

trim here →

* sandal

sandal x2 use the bottom of the feet with straps on top

sugar cane

* Parasol #6 oval

fold arms inward to hold parasol

right sleeve kimono *

left sleeve kimono *

* Kimono

follow pattern for sandals

* wooden shoes x2

top apron x2 *

#7 circle

* hair behind bangs or try using the skirt or bottom of hair

* bangs (boy's hair)

* Sash cheat the #7 rectangle

sandals x2

* hat

* tulips & leaves

apron

* cut here ↑

* cut here ↓

bottom layer of dress *

* pants

43

clogs

arms - follow template from shoulder to armpit, turn template to cheat at shoulder using the hand to round off.

cut off legs and position behind body

cut head out and place on body

arms

Flag
#1 cheated square

body and clothes

Flag Girl

Lounging Girl

arc of the foot facing left

#6 oval

arc of the heel facing left

shirt

shorts

Shift template up and continue around hand – connect to head with scissors at red dots

hand arc

Texas Flag

blue - #4 rectangle
star - #4 star
stripes - top and bottom of #1 heart

44

When making a custom paper doll, it helps to have a friend "model" for you.

frog foot
x2

Frog
body - #5 elongated oval
head - #7 elongated oval
legs - #8 elongated oval
eyes - hole punches

Lounging Boy
head - cut head to shoulders, turn template upside down and use top of head on template to complete circle.

body - slide template to achieve arm position, then use the sole of the foot to cheat when you get to the knee-caps (see page 9 method 4).

cut two left legs, place under knee caps

Can
#8 circle

worms

rectangle sides

boys

curve
of the crotch

hair

shirt

bow

Shirt

pants

foot

girl

curve of
the hand

shorts

tuck sides under
arms on each side

hair

shirt

cut hands
to here

stop
cutting
here

stop
cutting
here

1. cut head to shoulders
2. start at hands, use the hand
   curve at the elbows then
   continue down to armpit,
   follow pattern

foot curve

left
foot

left
foot

toe
curve

this foot
is not
attached
to body

shorts

toe
curve

hair

add 2 right
side ponytails

shirt pattern
(cut off sleeves
using waistline)

hair

tanktop - follow template

Boy and Pinwheel

bend

bend

mini scallop decorative scissors

*"slide" template to cut off legs

brim

hat top/head #8 oval

cut away and save for the pinwheel

#8 oval

hand cut 3 of these sections for pinwheel

if barefoot trim with mini scallop decorative scissors

any cheated rectangle

Boy and Train Tracks

*"slide" - see page 9, method 4
*"pivot" - see page 9, method 3

follow template for upper body, "slide" legs and position cross legged

upsidedown girl hair

scrap

scarf

*"pivot" hair down a tad and repeat

Overalls

square neck and follow body line

draw details with a milky white gel roller

Engineer Hat

top of girl hair

brim - top of head

track - #1 oval
slats - any square

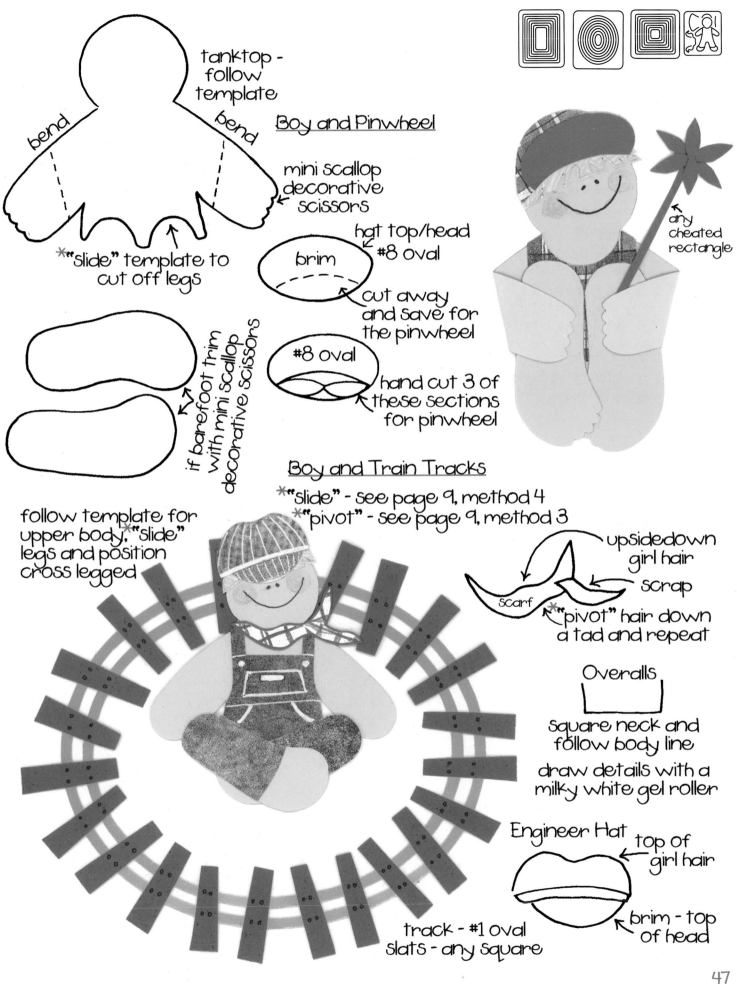

47

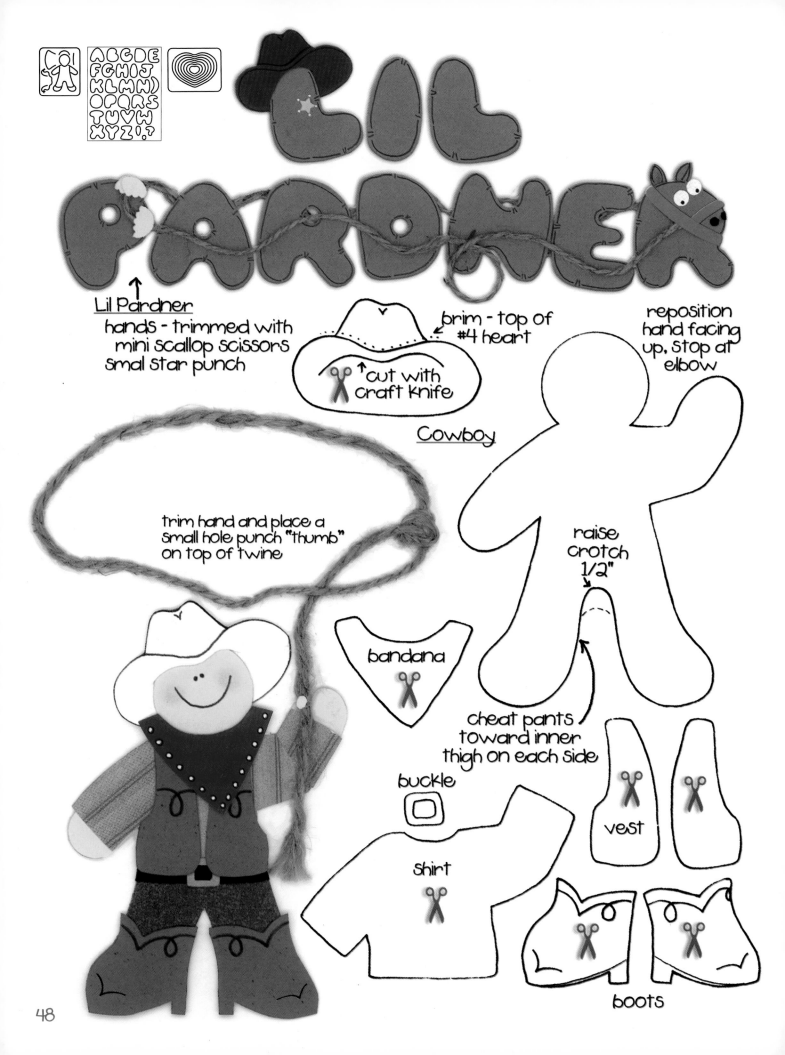

LIL PARDNER

Lil Pardner
hands - trimmed with mini scallop scissors small star punch

brim - top of #4 heart

cut with craft knife

Cowboy

reposition hand facing up, stop at elbow

trim hand and place a small hole punch "thumb" on top of twine

raise crotch 1/2"

bandana

cheat pants toward inner thigh on each side

buckle

vest

shirt

boots

48

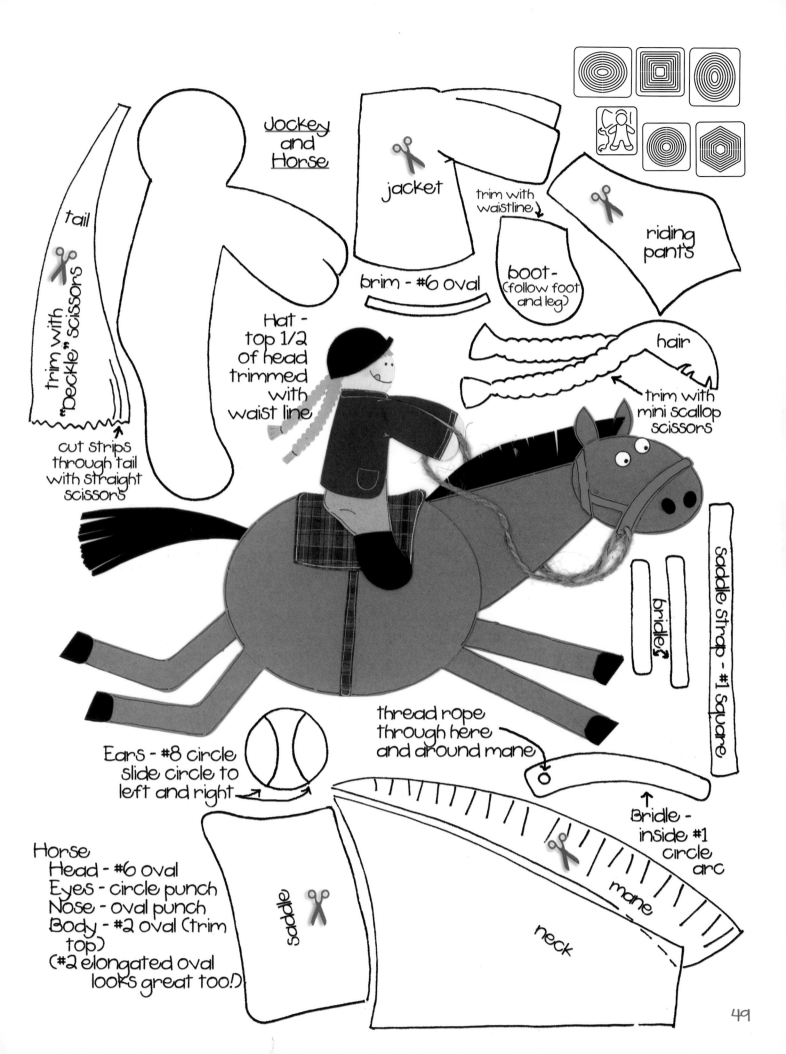

tail

trim with "beckle" scissors

cut strips through tail with straight scissors

Jockey and Horse

Hat - top 1/2 of head trimmed with waist line

jacket

brim - #6 oval

trim with waistline

boot - (follow foot and leg)

riding pants

hair

trim with mini scallop scissors

saddle strap - #1 square

bridles

Ears - #8 circle slide circle to left and right

thread rope through here and around mane

Bridle - inside #1 circle arc

saddle

mane

neck

Horse
  Head - #6 oval
  Eyes - circle punch
  Nose - oval punch
  Body - #2 oval (trim top)
  (#2 elongated oval looks great too!)

49

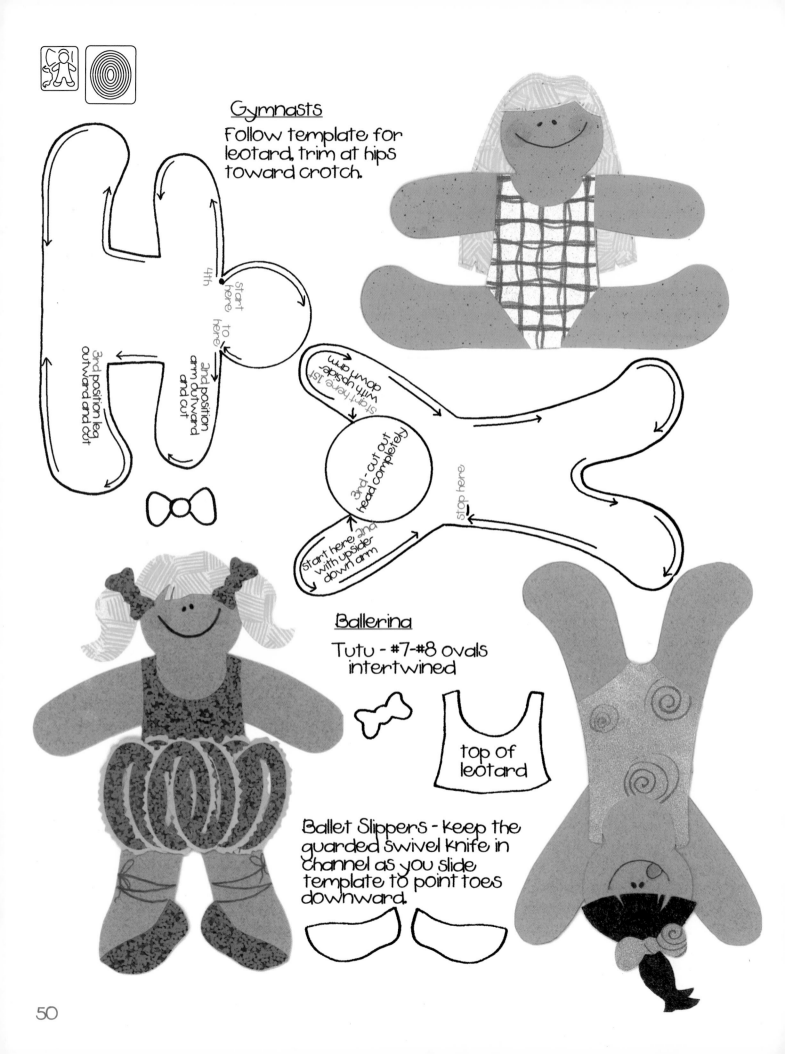

Gymnasts

Follow template for leotard, trim at hips toward crotch.

start here

to here

4th

2nd position arm outward and cut

3rd position leg outward and cut

Start here 1st with upside-down arm

3rd - cut out head completely

Start here 2nd with upsider down arm

stop here

Ballerina

Tutu - #7-#8 ovals intertwined

top of leotard

Ballet Slippers - keep the guarded swivel knife in channel as you slide template to point toes downward.

Golfer

hat ✂

Shirt ✂ — draw this detail

tuck under left leg

right leg ✂

cut off head

golfer's left pant leg ✂

saddle shoes x2

bend here

after you fold, cut here and bend doll over a little

pull arm template up a little to make shorter

Tennis Racket

strings - #6 oval - adhere to purple cardstock and hand trim 1/8" around strings
handle - #1 cheated square
hand draw strings with a black pen

Club - bottom of doll hand and arm handle of club - rectangle

Tennis Ball Can
top and bottom - #1 elongated oval
sides - rectangle

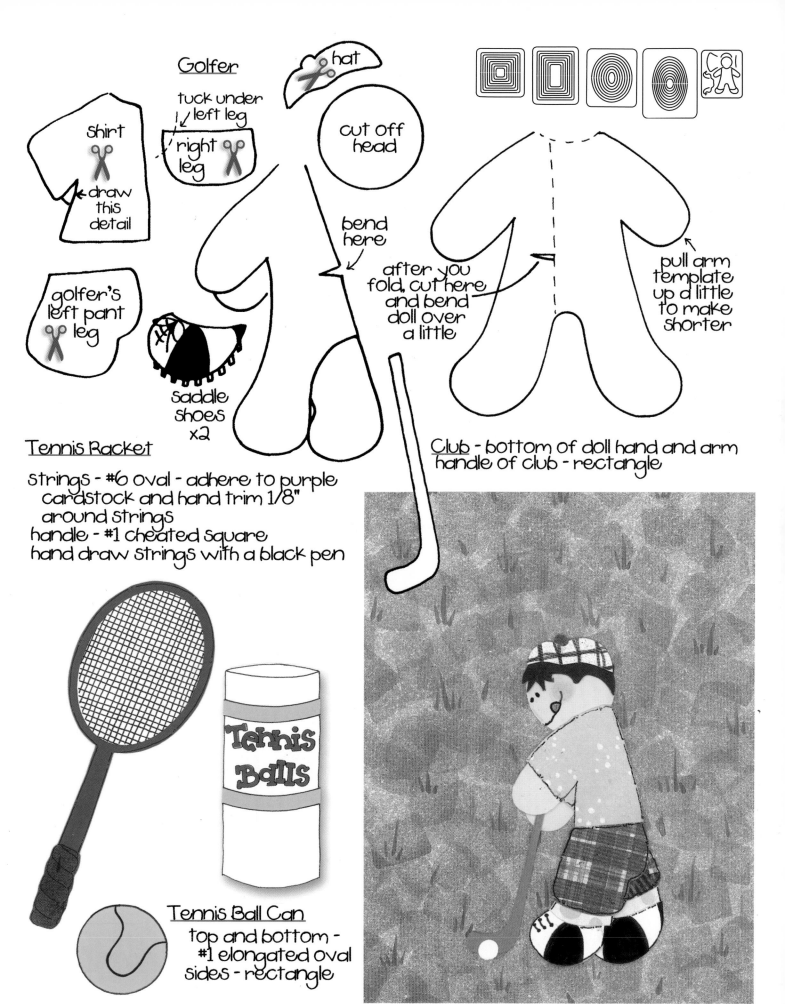

51

frame behind hoop

connect here

head

Jersey

right side of body

Waistline

#7-#8 square trimmed

#4 circle

Backboard

#4 rectangle bottom

Waistline

Shorts

#7 cheated square

Hoop

follow pattern

Net

2nd - cut this arm

1st cut head

don't cut all the way

3rd - cut

4th - twist arm up and cut

5th - right side of doll

7th - right side of doll

Make a bend in knee by twisting the template

8th - cut foot

6th - cut foot, now attach

23

23

shoes - use foot

GO TEAM!!

ABCDE
FGHIJ
KLMN]
OPQRS
TUVW
XYZ!.?

girl's skirt ✂

girl's top ✂

Girl Cheerleader
position and cut:
1 - head
2 - right arm
3 - side of body
4 - right leg
5 - left leg
6 - side of body
7 - left arm

✂ 🎀

When dressing a custom positioned paper doll, try using the doll you've cut as a template for the clothes. Put doll on top of paper and cut slightly larger around it. Trim here & there and you've got a great fit!

boy's pants

cheat toward the center on inside pant legs

boy's sweater ✂

Boy Cheerleader
position and cut:
1 - both arms up (touching)
2 - rest of body excluding head
3 - head, turn template and continue
attach clothing,
place head in front of arms

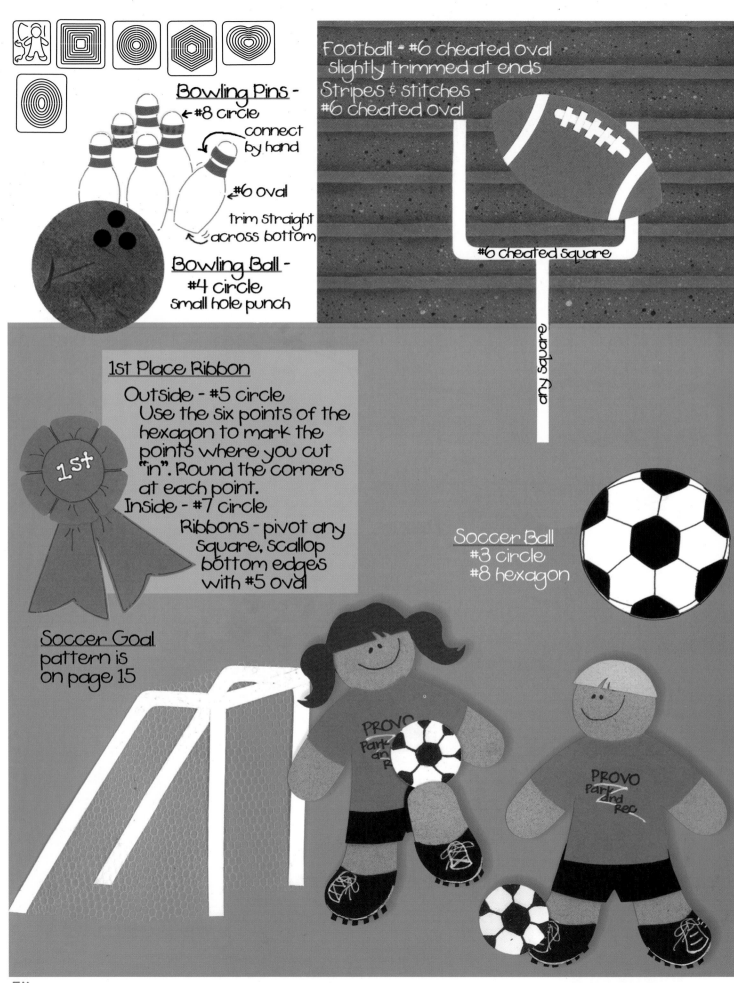

Bowling Pins -
← #8 circle

connect by hand

#6 oval

trim straight across bottom

Bowling Ball -
#4 circle
small hole punch

Football - #6 cheated oval
slightly trimmed at ends
Stripes & stitches -
#6 cheated oval

#6 cheated square

any square

1st Place Ribbon

Outside - #5 circle
Use the six points of the hexagon to mark the points where you cut "in". Round the corners at each point.
Inside - #7 circle
Ribbons - pivot any square, scallop bottom edges with #5 oval

Soccer Ball
#3 circle
#8 hexagon

Soccer Goal
pattern is on page 15

1st

PROVO
Park and Rec

PROVO
Park and Rec

When making just a head, (to "peek" over titles or pictures), cut from shoulder to shoulder across head, then turn template upside down, match cuts and continue cutting around neck with top of template head.

Patterns on pages 56 & 57

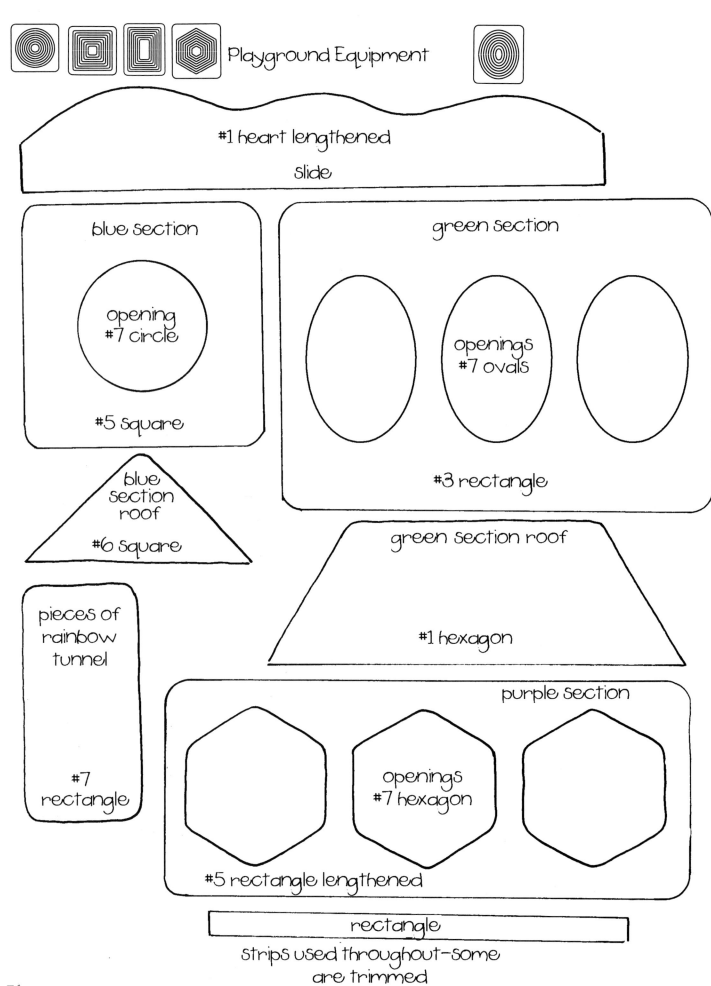

Playground Equipment

#1 heart lengthened

Slide

blue section

opening
#7 circle

#5 square

green section

openings
#7 ovals

#3 rectangle

blue
section
roof

#6 square

green section roof

#1 hexagon

pieces of
rainbow
tunnel

#7
rectangle

purple section

openings
#7 hexagon

#5 rectangle lengthened

rectangle

Strips used throughout—some
are trimmed

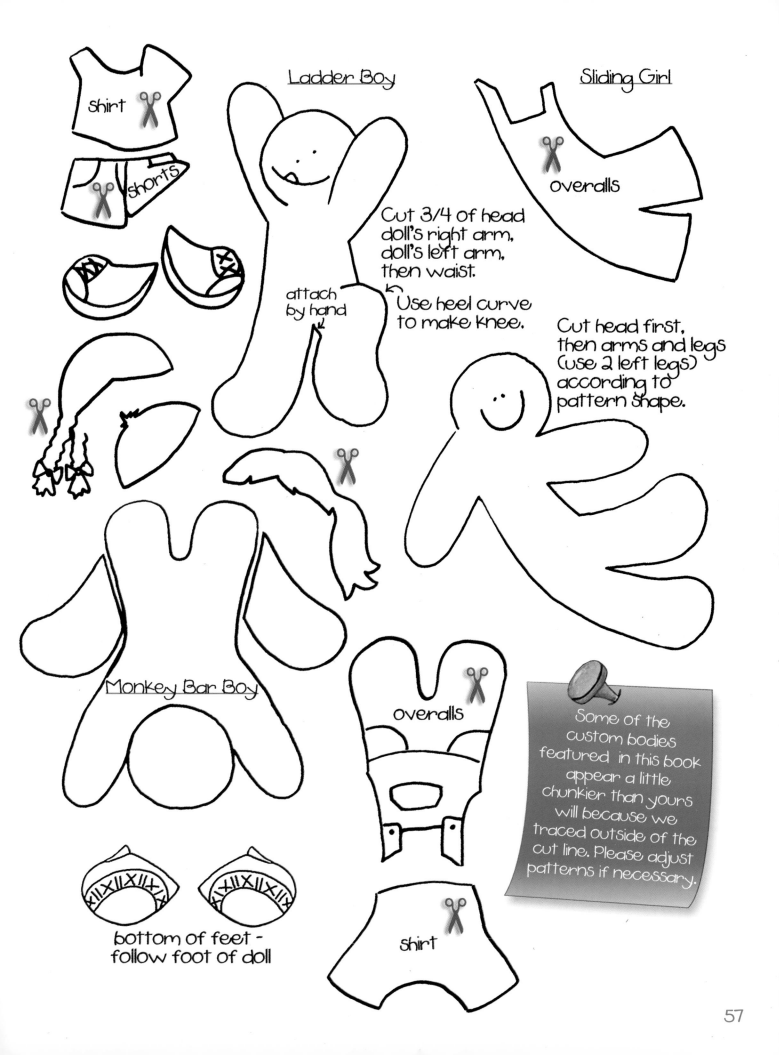

shirt

shorts

Ladder Boy

Sliding Girl

overalls

Cut 3/4 of head
doll's right arm,
doll's left arm,
then waist.

attach
by hand

Use heel curve
to make knee.

Cut head first,
then arms and legs
(use 2 left legs)
according to
pattern shape.

Monkey Bar Boy

overalls

Some of the
custom bodies
featured in this book
appear a little
chunkier than yours
will because we
traced outside of the
cut line. Please adjust
patterns if necessary.

bottom of feet -
follow foot of doll

shirt

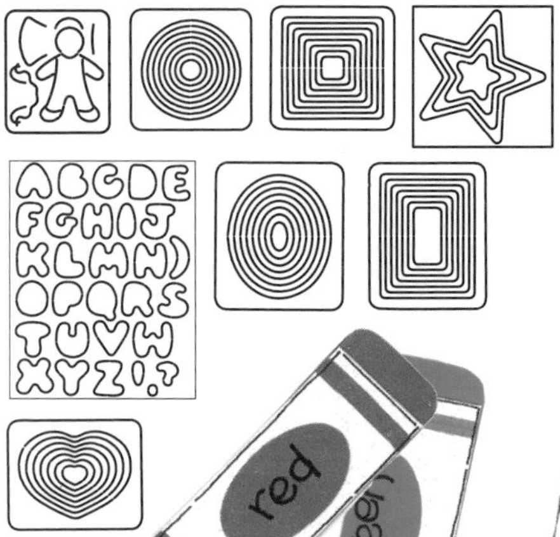

TEACHER'S PET

chalkboard -
#1 cheated rectangle

apple - #4 heart
leaf - #7 cheated circle

beret
#6 oval

desk -
#7 cheated rectangle

hand - trim
with mini
scallop
scissors

chair -
#7 rectangle

Shirt

ABC frame -
#4-#5 cheated square
chalkboard -
#5 cheated square

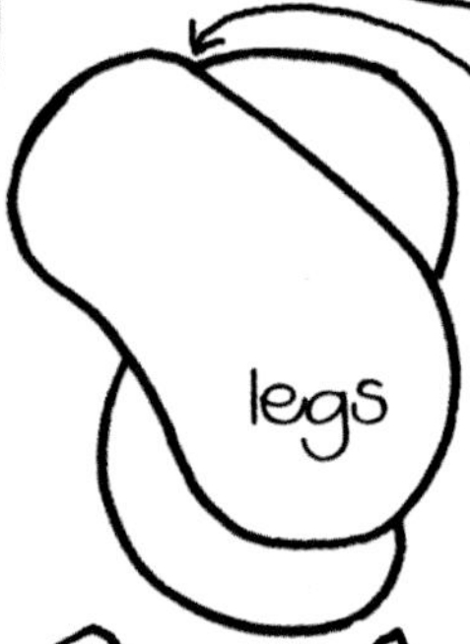

use the foot
to close
off the knee

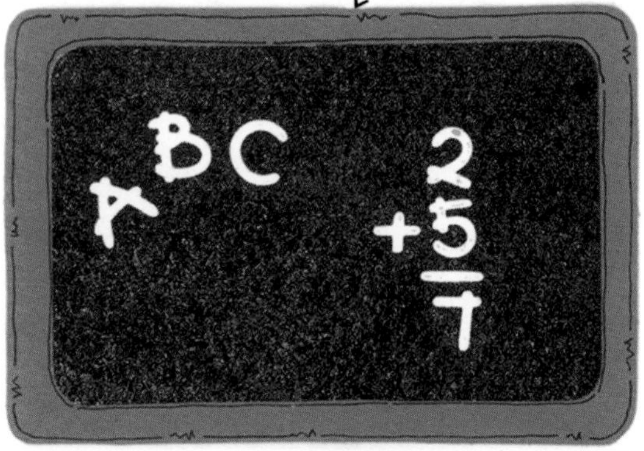

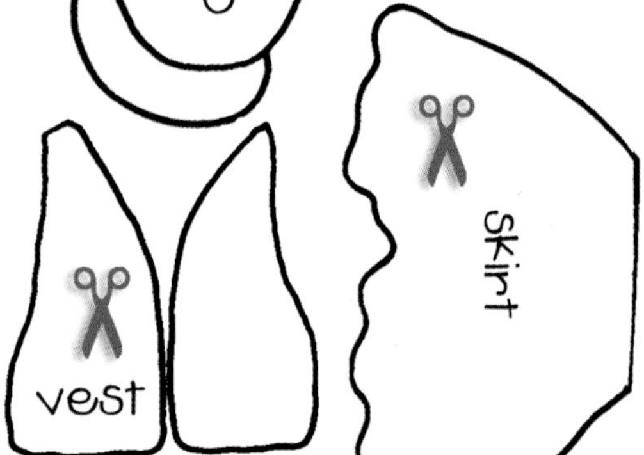

legs

Skirt

vest

A B C   2
          +5
          ―
          7

penny
loafers

red

Green

Purple

blue

yellow

School Bus

Try converting a crayon into a <u>Pencil</u>

Crayon

black
brown
trim with
deckle
decorative
scissors
silver
yellow
pink

#1 star point cut off tip

center label
#8 oval

#7 cheated rectangle

trim here for white wrapper

"Scrapbook" Alphabitties

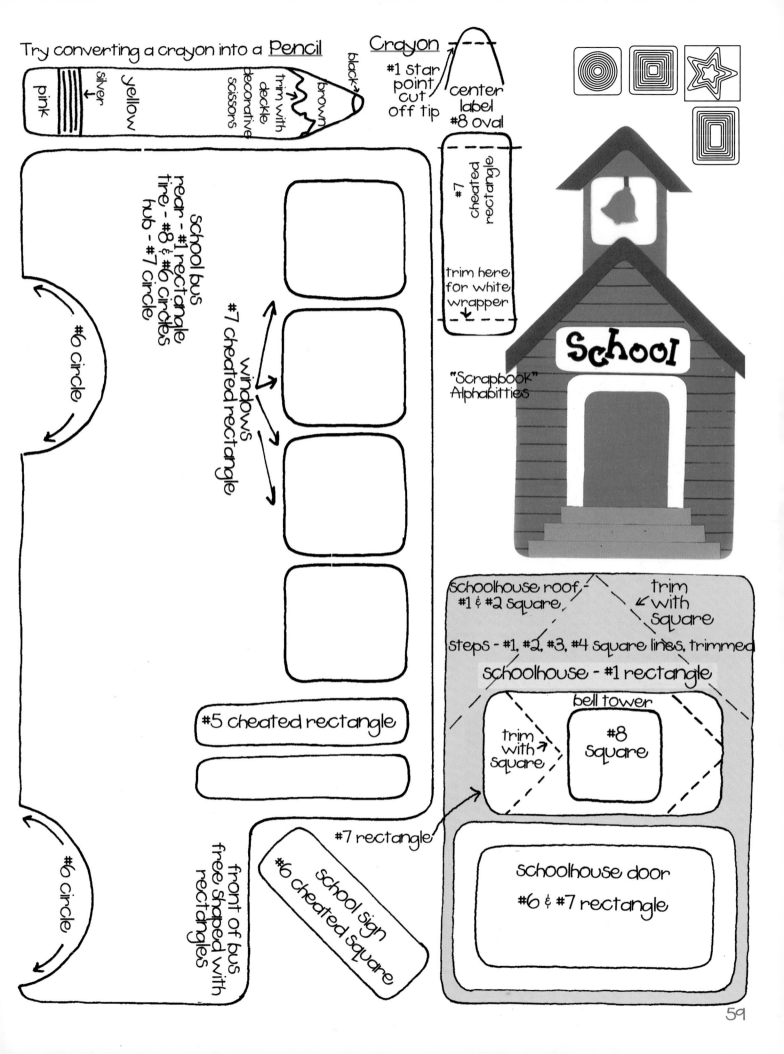

School

school bus
rear - #1 rectangle
tire - #8 & #6 circles
hub - #7 circle

windows
#7 cheated rectangle

#6 circle

#5 cheated rectangle

#6 circle

front of bus
free shaped with rectangles

school sign
#6 cheated square

#7 rectangle

Schoolhouse roof - #1 & #2 square

trim with square

Steps - #1, #2, #3, #4 square lines, trimmed

schoolhouse - #1 rectangle

bell tower
trim with square
#8 square

schoolhouse door
#6 & #7 rectangle

Web - Sketch web on back of paper. Use straight edges of square and curves from circle or oval to cut around pencil lines.
IMPORTANT: keep the web in one piece, don't cut where drawn lines cross.

Bat
    wings - #2 oval trimmed with #8 circles
    body - #6 oval
    head - #7 circle

"Spooky" Bats
    body - #8 oval
    wings - #8 circle with #8 oval cut outs

Moon - #3 circle
    inside - #5 circle

Spider - #8 circle
    legs - #2 pivoted heart

Frankenstein
    head - #6 square
    body - #5 square
    hands - #8 circle
    arms - #4 cheated square

Mummy
    head - #6 circle
    body - #5 circle
    arms - #1-#3 circle, rounded at bottom with #8 circle

60

Pumpkin Costume

#5 circles

1/2   1/2

Hands
trim with
mini scallop
decorative
scissors

cut tip
of handcut
off at wrist

stem

Leaves
#8 circles

shoe
x2

Pumpkin -
#6 oval (3)

Spider Costume
legs (8) - #5 cheated circle
body - #5 circle
eyes - circle hole punch
hourglass - #8 square

---- fold   cut along
                 dotted line

Witch's Feet
#1-#3 square or
rectangle
#1 oval (top) hand
cut heel

Headband - is top of
head, move template
down 1/4", cut top
of head again

bangs

hair - continue
down from girl
hair, cut off
ponytails

Crab -
use spider costume instructions (with 2
    eyes and 6 legs)
claw - #7 circle with 1/4 section cut out

Acorn and Oak Leaves

Leaves - #6 oval
trim leaves with "Big Cut" scissors

#8 oval

#7 heart

leaves

Hand trim "turkey leg" alphabet, after cutting from Coluzzle® alphabet template.

I'M STUFFED

Wing - cut 4, #6 elongated ovals, trimming
each one differently, then layer

Turkey

Feather

#8 oval

straight edge
of square

Beak
Star punch
trimmed

Waddle
#8 pivoted
oval

#3 heart

turkey
body

cut here for lower
(purple) portion of
body

Gingerbread House

house - #1 square lengthened
roof - #1 & #4 square trimmed with
  Big Cut decorative scissors
chimney - #7 rectangle
snow on chimney - #6 rectangle
  trimmed
doorway - #6 and #7 rectangle
mints - #8 circles
gumdrops - #8 oval

gum drop

Gingerbread Boy

1 - trace the head
2 - rotate and cut arms
  upward like he's going
  to give you a hug.
3 - the legs are the tricky
  part - they have to be
  positioned closer to each
  other than they are on the
  template. Bring them up
  and closer together; cut.
  buttons - star punch

Gingerbread Girl

1 - follow gingerbread boy
  steps 1 & 2.
2 - bring dress bottom up,
  trim just to legs.
3 - cut legs under dress
  (see gingerbread girl)
buttons - heart punch
*use wavy scissors for gingerbread accents

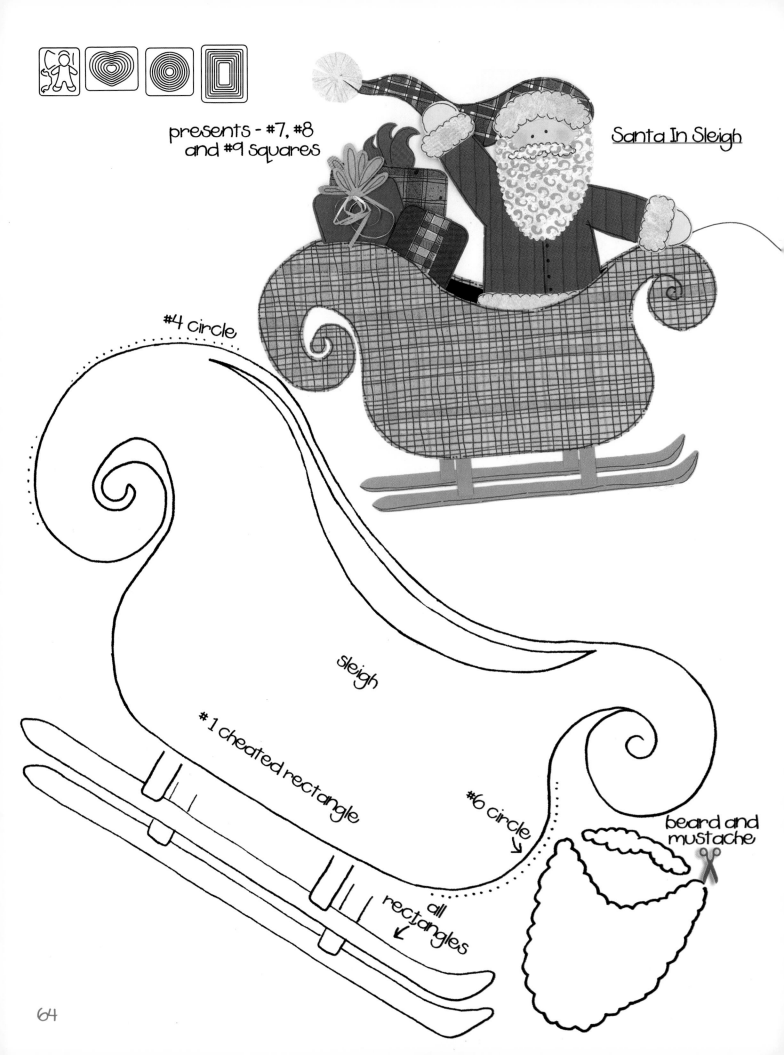

presents - #7, #8
and #9 squares

Santa In Sleigh

#4 circle

sleigh

#1 cheated rectangle

#6 circle

beard and
mustache

all
rectangles

64

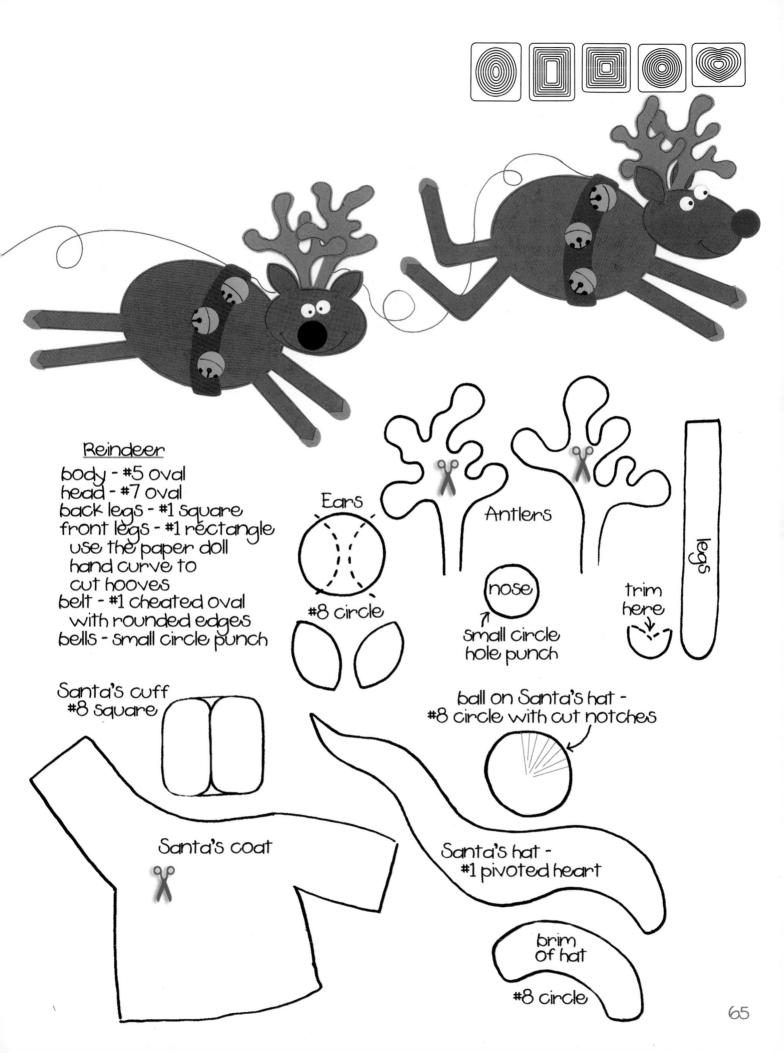

Reindeer

body - #5 oval
head - #7 oval
back legs - #1 square
front legs - #1 rectangle
  use the paper doll
  hand curve to
  cut hooves
belt - #1 cheated oval
  with rounded edges
bells - small circle punch

Ears

#8 circle

Antlers

nose
↑
small circle
hole punch

legs

trim
here

Santa's cuff
#8 square

Santa's coat

ball on Santa's hat -
#8 circle with cut notches

Santa's hat -
#1 pivoted heart

brim
of hat

#8 circle

Wreath

outside - #1 circle
inside - #6 circle
trim with decorative scissors
child's face and hair - #5 circle
bow - #6 heart

bow
center
#8
circle

#1 pivoted
circle x2

Do Not Open 'til Christmas

Christmas Tag
#6 square
#6 hexagon

santa
hat

#2 star

#6 heart
cut out for face

#2 star

Star Santa

face - #6 circle
   (place behind cut out heart)
eyebrow - #9 elongated oval (trimmed)
hatband - #7 cheated square

mustache - #3 cheated heart

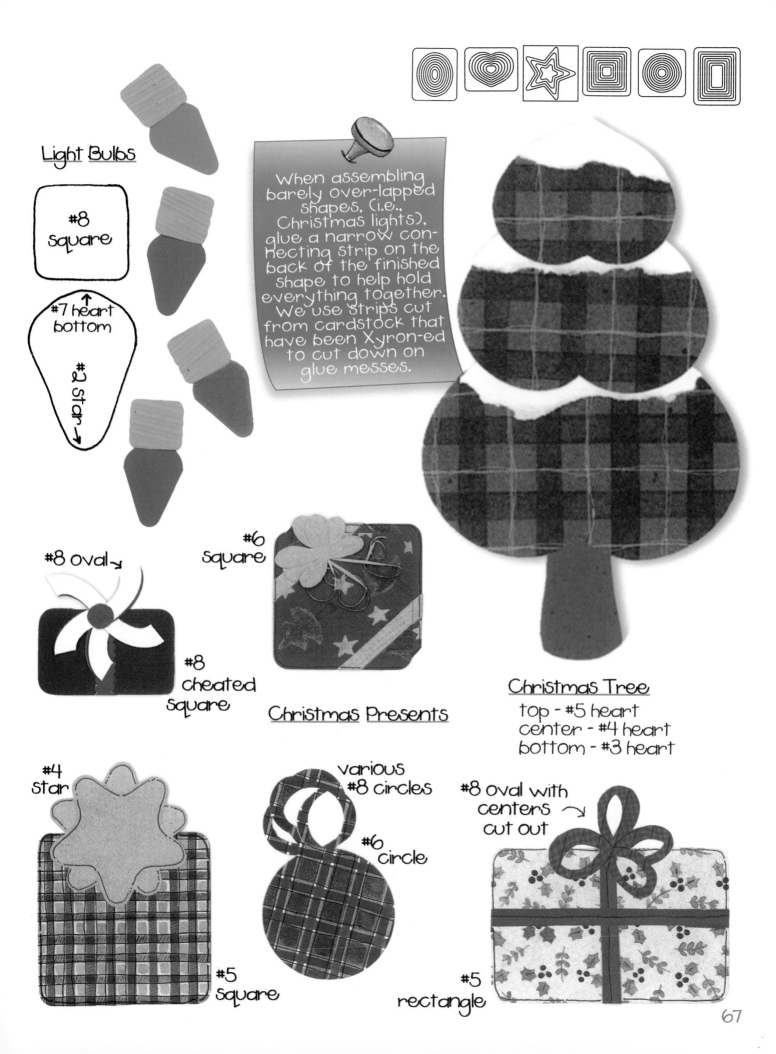

Light Bulbs

#8 square

#7 heart bottom
#2 star

When assembling barely over-lapped shapes, (i.e., Christmas lights), glue a narrow connecting strip on the back of the finished shape to help hold everything together. We use strips cut from cardstock that have been Xyron-ed to cut down on glue messes.

#8 oval

#8 cheated square

#6 square

Christmas Presents

Christmas Tree
top - #5 heart
center - #4 heart
bottom - #3 heart

#4 star

#5 square

various #8 circles

#6 circle

#5 square

#8 oval with centers cut out

#5 rectangle

67

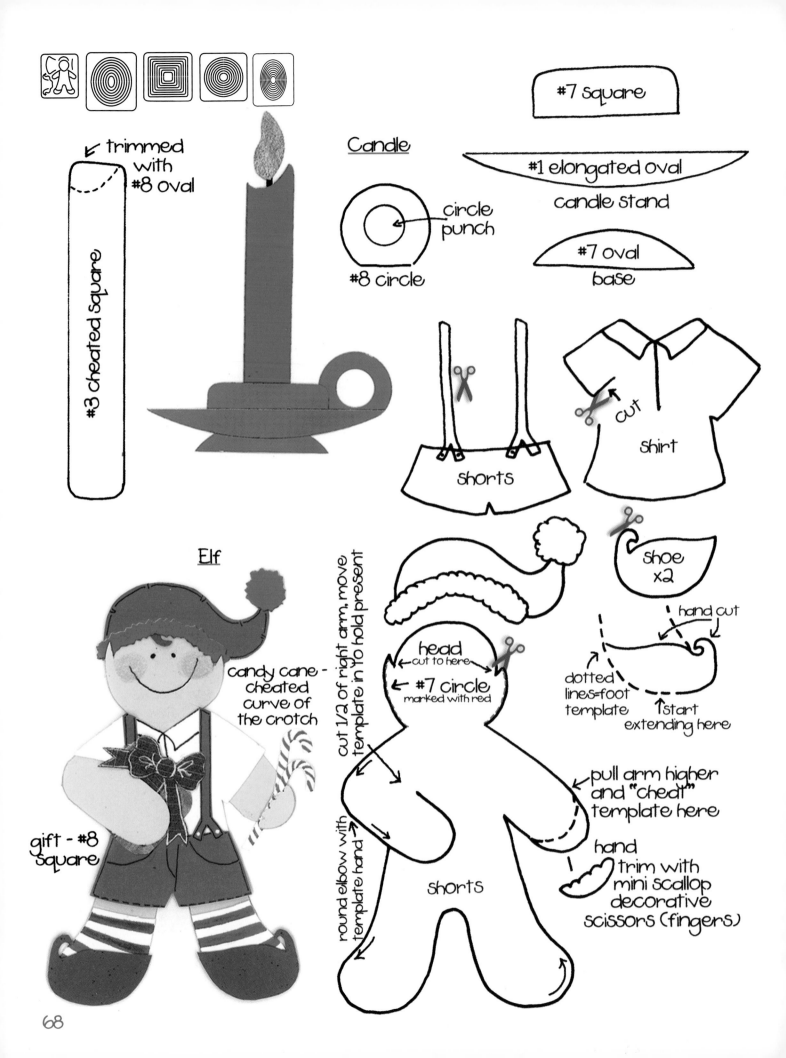

trimmed with #8 oval

#3 cheated square

Candle

circle punch

#8 circle

#7 square

#1 elongated oval
candle stand

#7 oval
base

Shorts

cut

Shirt

shoe x2

hand cut

dotted lines=foot template

start extending here

Elf

candy cane – cheated curve of the crotch

gift – #8 square

cut ½ of right arm, move template in to hold present

head
cut to here

#7 circle
marked with red

round elbow with template hand

pull arm higher and "cheat" template here

hand
trim with mini scallop decorative scissors (fingers)

Shorts

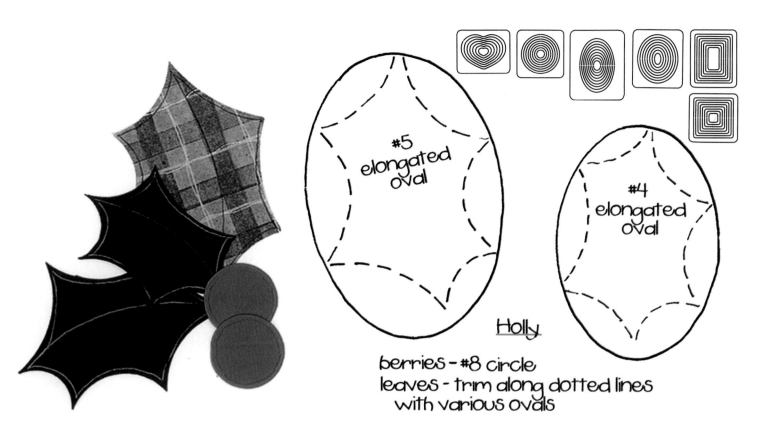

#5 elongated oval

#4 elongated oval

Holly

berries – #8 circle
leaves – trim along dotted lines
with various ovals

Toy Soldier

head – #6 circle
legs – #6 cheated rectangle
shoes – #7 hearts

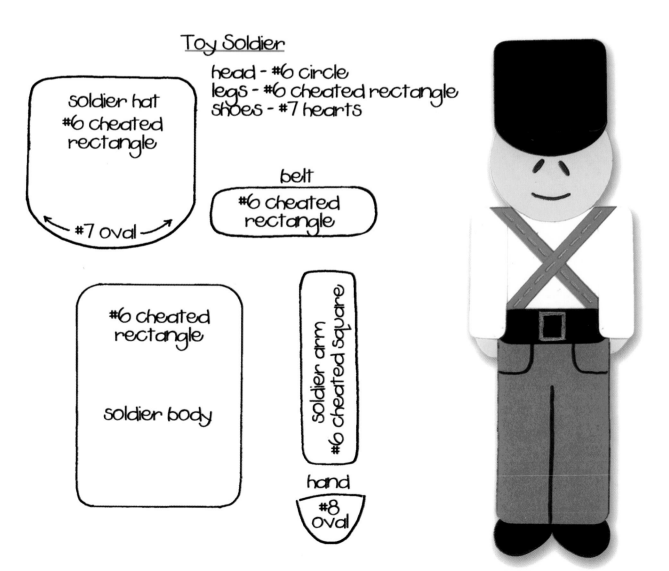

soldier hat
#6 cheated rectangle

← #7 oval →

belt
#6 cheated rectangle

#6 cheated rectangle

soldier body

soldier arm
#6 cheated square

hand
#8 oval

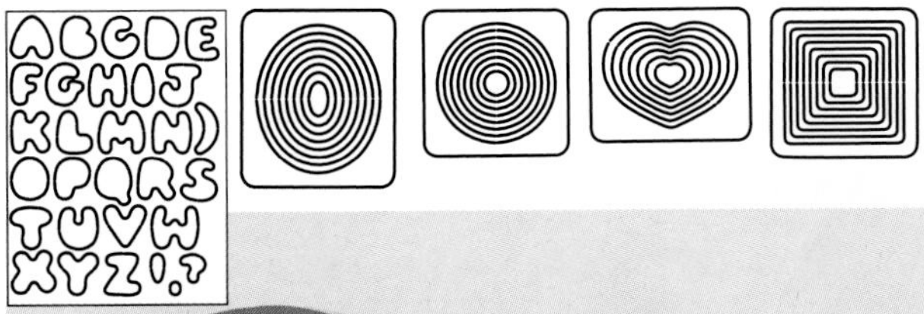

ANGELS

"Angels" Alphabet Template
halo outside - #8 oval
halo inside - #8 cheated oval

Clouds
do your own thing with
various ovals and circles

arm
#1 oval &
any
square
or
rectangle

halo
#6 - #7 oval
(cut #7 oval
slightly
off center)

Angel

head
#5 circle

body
#1 oval

wings
#2 heart

hands
#8 oval

hair
#3 heart
(round off point)

bangs
#5 circle
(trimmed)

Trim with mini scallop scissors then put a teeny hole punch in each scallop

ponytail curve twice

wing x2

#6 heart

connect this section with scissors

halo - #8 cheated oval (round ends)

bangs - girl hair
hair - girl hair lengthened downward with curve of crotch flip

lengthen dress

oval punch

doll template body

#2 heart

hair

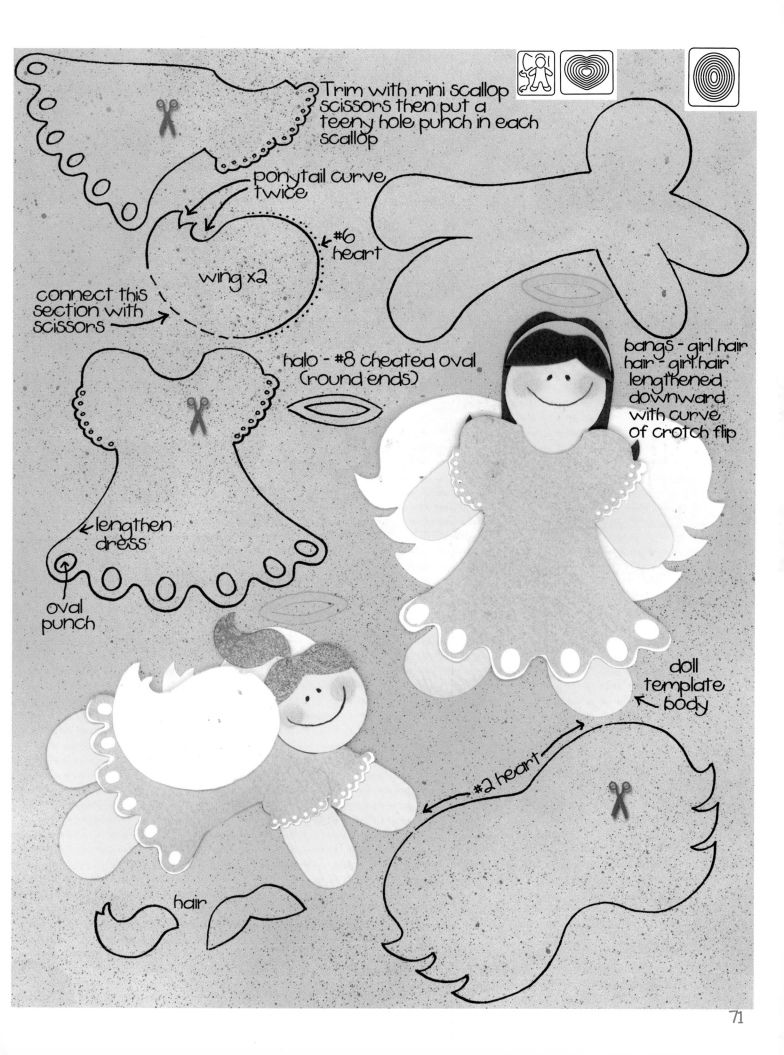

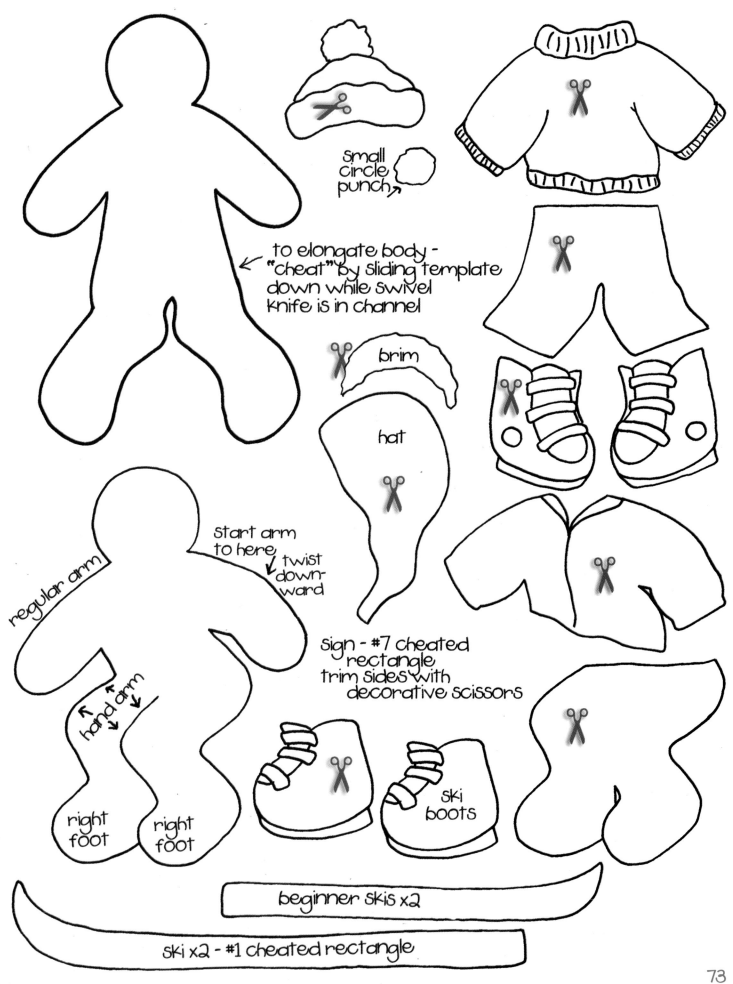

small circle punch

to elongate body – "cheat" by sliding template down while swivel knife is in channel

brim

hat

regular arm

start arm to here

twist down-ward

hand arm

right foot

right foot

sign – #7 cheated rectangle trim sides with decorative scissors

ski boots

beginner skis x2

ski x2 – #1 cheated rectangle

73

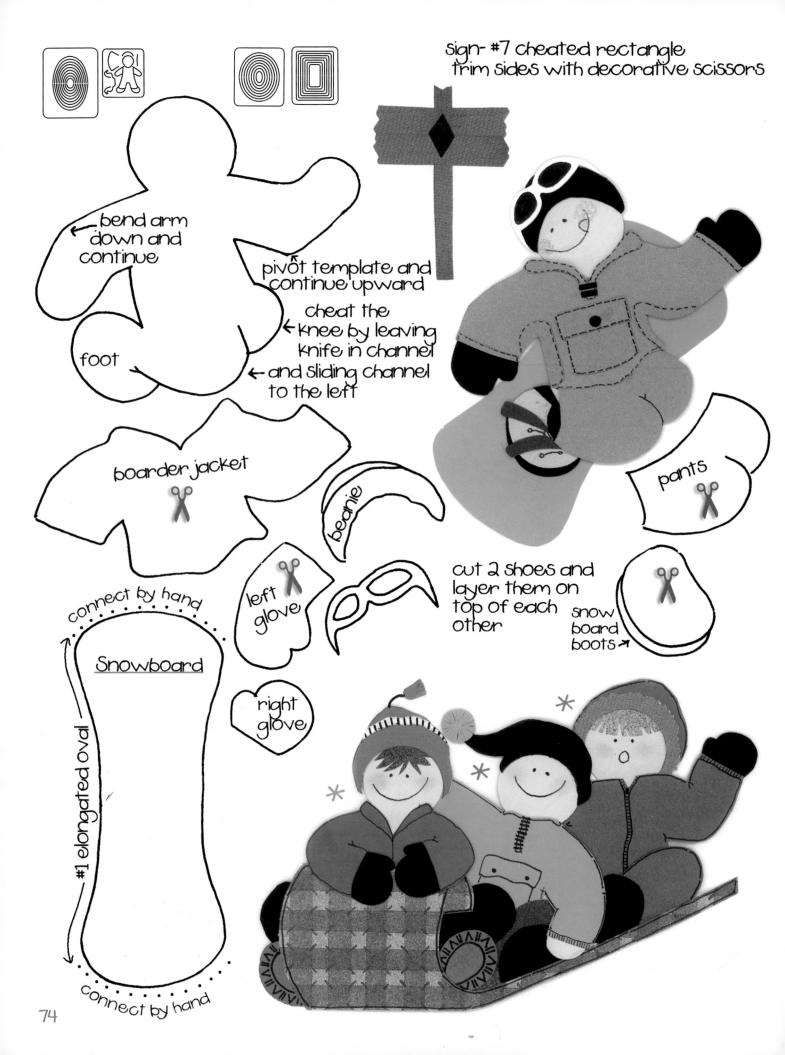

sign- #7 cheated rectangle
trim sides with decorative scissors

bend arm
down and
continue

pivot template and
continue upward

cheat the
knee by leaving
knife in channel

foot

and sliding channel
to the left

boarder jacket ✂

beanie

pants ✂

left glove ✂

cut 2 shoes and
layer them on
top of each
other

snow
board
boots →

✂

connect by hand

Snowboard

right glove

#1 elongated oval

connect by hand

74

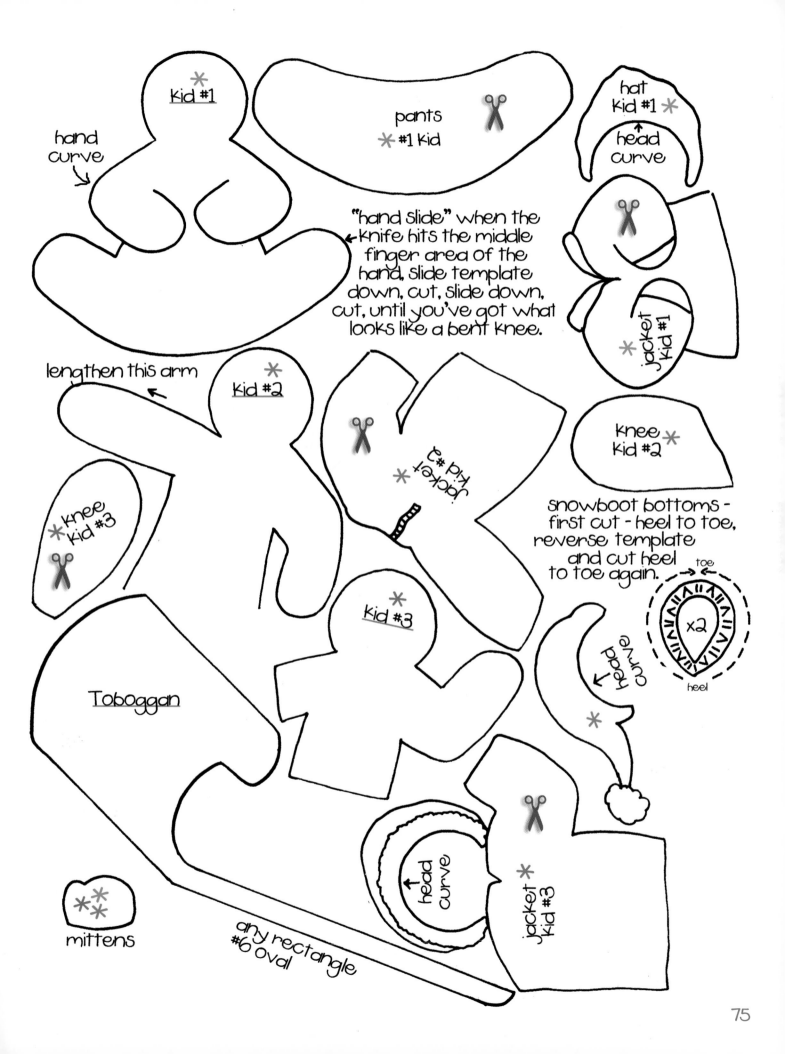

Kid #1

hand
curve

pants
#1 Kid

hat
Kid #1

head
curve

"hand slide" when the
knife hits the middle
finger area of the
hand, slide template
down, cut, slide down,
cut, until you've got what
looks like a bent knee.

jacket
Kid #1

knee
Kid #2

lengthen this arm

Kid #2

jacket
kid #3

snowboot bottoms -
first cut - heel to toe,
reverse template
and cut heel
to toe again.

knee
Kid #3

toe

x2

heel

Toboggan

Kid #3

head
curve

head
curve

mittens

any rectangle
#6 oval

jacket
Kid #3

penguin scarf ✂

To achieve that "torn" look cut a shape with any Coluzzle®, then dip the outside edges in water. Now tear off the edges.

nose ✂

✂ foot x 2

Penguin
body - #2 oval
tummy - #3 oval
head - #6 circle
face - #7 circle
wings - #4 oval

Snow Globe - #3 circle
base - #3 hexagon

Eskimo
body - #1 oval   head - # 5 circle
arms #1 oval   hands - #8 circle
hood - #2 & #6 circle   cuffs - #7 square
trim hood and cuffs with decorative scissors

Fireplace - #3 rectangle
flames -various pivoted hearts
logs - #6 cheated rectangle
inside of fireplace - #4 rectangle
(placed higher toward top)

76

Nose

Add this bunny head to the animal bodies on page 30 to make a full size bunny.

#3 cheated ovals

Ears #5 cheated ovals

#5 circle

Bunny

Bunny head

Paws #8 oval (trimmed)

#4 circle

any rectangle

#3 oval

Magician's Hat top

#7 cheated rectangle

cut and place the bottom of hat through slit

discard

Magician's hat rim - #8 cheated oval, use same oval to cut slit

bow tie

Magician

Rim of large hat

#1 oval

#3 oval

suit

lapel

white shirt

pants - cheat inward on both sides

77

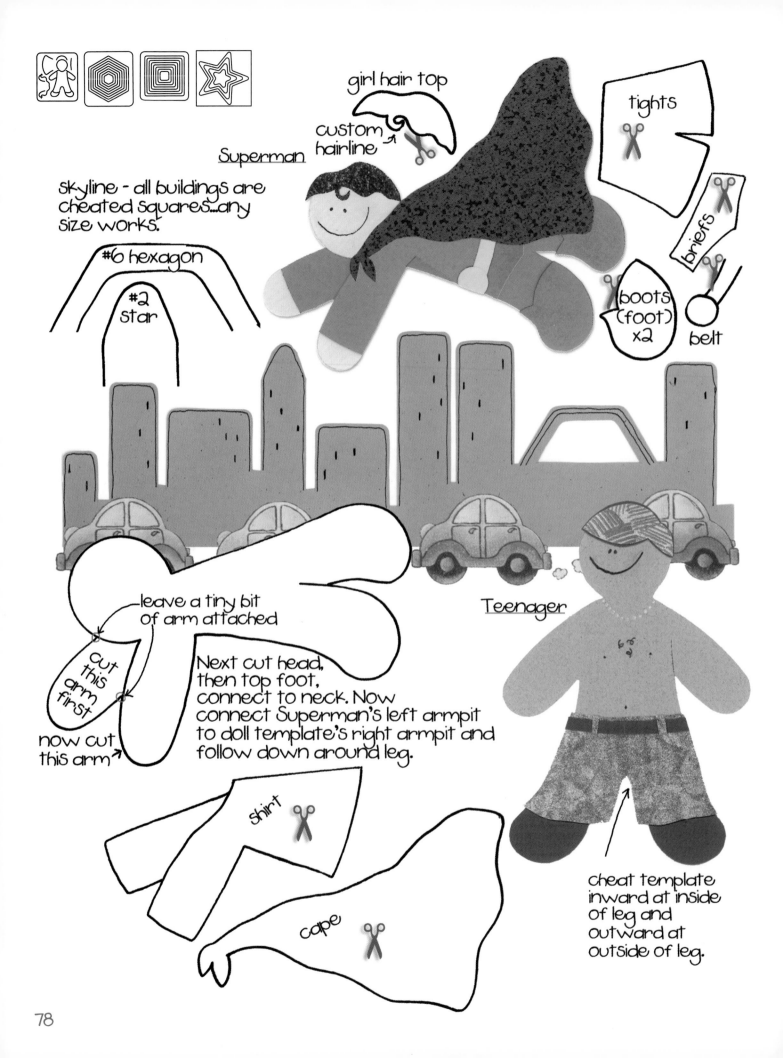

girl hair top

custom hairline

tights ✂

Superman

skyline - all buildings are cheated squares...any size works.

#6 hexagon

#2 star

briefs ✂

boots (foot) x2

belt

leave a tiny bit of arm attached

cut this arm first

now cut this arm →

Next cut head, then top foot, connect to neck. Now connect Superman's left armpit to doll template's right armpit and follow down around leg.

Teenager

shirt ✂

cape ✂

cheat template inward at inside of leg and outward at outside of leg.

PIZZA

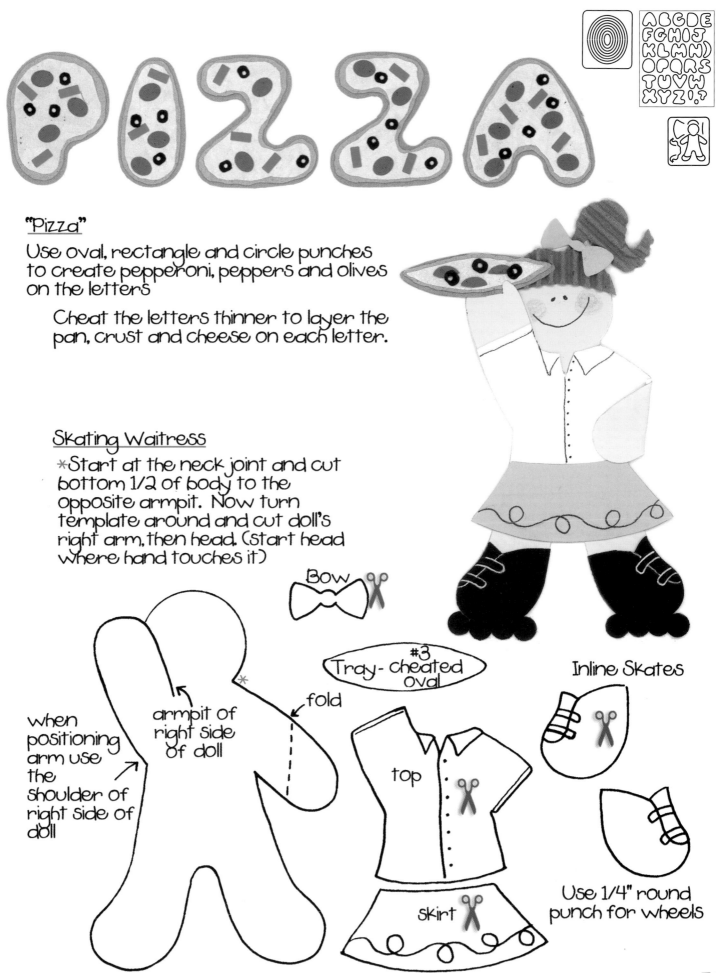

"Pizza"

Use oval, rectangle and circle punches to create pepperoni, peppers and olives on the letters

Cheat the letters thinner to layer the pan, crust and cheese on each letter.

Skating Waitress

*Start at the neck joint and cut bottom 1/2 of body to the opposite armpit. Now turn template around and cut doll's right arm, then head. (Start head where hand touches it)

Bow

Tray- cheated oval #3

Inline Skates

fold

when positioning arm use the shoulder of right side of doll

armpit of right side of doll

top

skirt

Use 1/4" round punch for wheels

SIPPIN' SODA

two ponytails

cut elbow with #6 oval and place on body

bend

use square for straw

#1 elongated oval

cut with #1 elongated oval stop just short of edge of glass

cut here for liquid

Ice cube

#8 square

Glass of lemonade

#5 rectangle pivoted slightly outward

Cut out two dolls extending the arms by 1/2". Use waistline to cut off boy's right arm.
Hand & fingers - use cut off arms, round off the fingers with mini scallop scissors.
Clothes - use doll template, cheat pants inward on each inner thigh.

this side up²

Cafe booth (bottom)

#1 cheated square

Cafe booth (top)

#1 cheated square

Table top - cheated **#5 rectangle**

Table pedestal square

Table bottom cheated square

shorten bodies to make dolls "sit"

Happy Birthday

hat - #1 star template (trimmed)

#1 oval

trim round punch

for party hat

#4 circle

#5 circle

#5 oval

#7 heart

Balloons

White Birthday Cake
layers - #1 & #2 cheated squares
frosting - #1 cheated squares,
trimmed with decorative scissors

round down birthday
girl's arms to fingers
← hands

trim with mini
scallop scissors

Birthday Party

all clothes
are on doll
template
except for
"V" necks

Chocolate Birthday Cake

#7 square

hand cut

#7 cheated
square

MOVIE NIGHT

#5 pivoted oval

Admit One
Admit One

#6 oval
#7 oval
#6 oval
#5 oval
#7 oval
#6 oval
#5 pivoted oval

Popcorn

Movie Reel

Step 1 - Cut a #1 circle out of extra paper and trace around it on cardstock.

Step 2 - Use #2 hexagon to divide traced circle into sixths. Don't cut! Just use your knife point to barely pierce paper at points of hexagon. Connect points with pencil (red dashed lines).

Step 3 - Using tip of #1 star, cut each section (black dashed lines) stopping 1/4" from edge of circle (may be traced first, then cut).

Step 4 - Using #2 circle finish cut begun with star.

Step 5 - Use #1 circle to cut on traced line.

Step 6 - Use hand punch to add center of reel.

To achieve a "ribbon" look cut outer portion of curve with a smaller oval than the inner curve.

"Scrapbook" Alphabitties
MOVIE TICKET
#7 rectangle

← trim with decorative scissors
circle punch

#1 circle
#2 circle

#1 star

Circle hole punch

Rectangle hole punch

Reel

Popcorn Bag

Label - #7 elongated oval

Popcorn

#7 heart

#9 oval

#7 heart

#4 rectangle trimmed with "pinking" decorative scissors

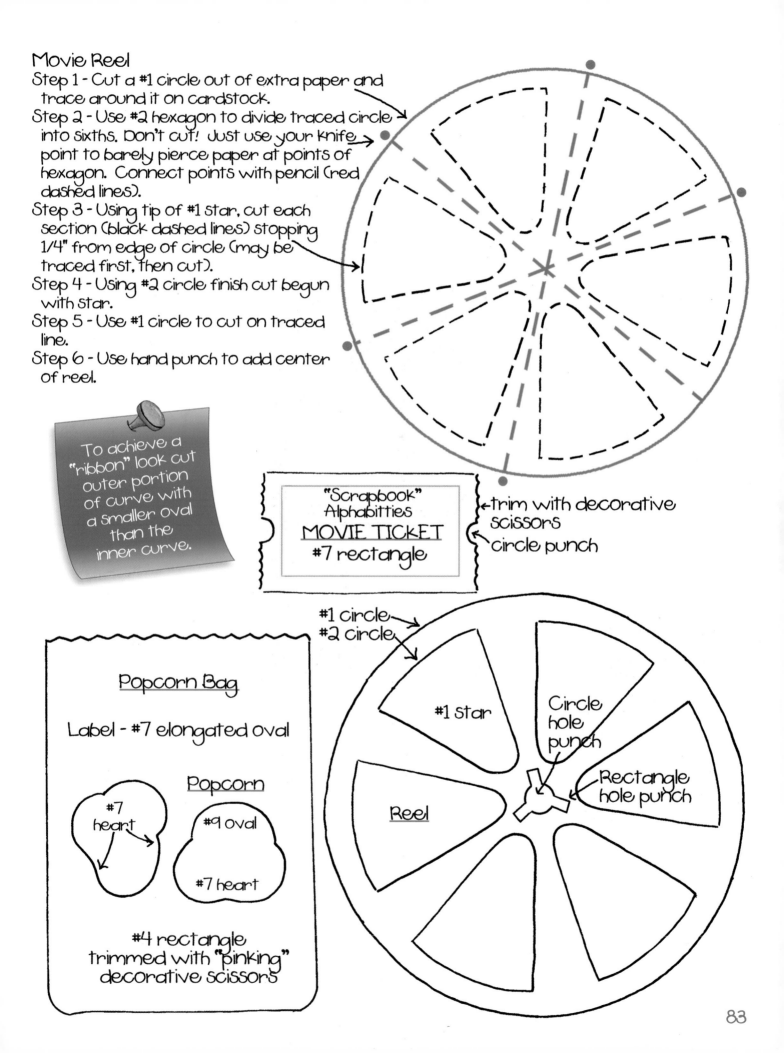

bride's hair

bride

groom

trim hands with mini scallop scissors

wedding ring - "cheat" with mini scallop scissors

cut bottom of foot then hand cut to heel

groom's shoes

both sides are the bottom of the foot

Glass
cup - #5 oval
base - #5 circle

#8 oval

Stained Glass Window
back with different
colored paper

#1 oval
#2 oval
#4 oval
#5 oval
#5 oval
#4 oval
#3 oval
#1 oval

cut all ovals without moving the oval template

cheated rectangle

gem

Rings -
#6 circle

cut
gem
from
a square
punch

Music Notes
any rectangle
#8 circle
cheated rectangle →

Church Steeple
make a church out
of the school house,
(page 59) by
adding steeple in
place of bell tower

cross
punch

#2 star

#6 cheated
rectangle

base -
#7 rectangle
trimmed
with
square
on
bottom

Car
body, bumper & lights -
  #2 cheated rectangle
license plate - #8 cheated square
"Kids" Alphabitties

Just Married

WAHOO!

85

FOUR WHEELIN'

girl

boy

girl's hair

boy's hair

Hand - trimmed on both sides with mini scallop scissors

Antennae - #1 oval with hole punch dot on top (cheat #1 oval inward)

Convertible -
dash - #1 hexagon
top of car - #1-#2 hexagon
body of car - #3 cheated rectangle
lights - #8 slightly cheated square
grill - #7 rectangle
steering wheel - #7-#8 circle
tires - #7 cheated rectangle (use zig-zag scissors for tread)

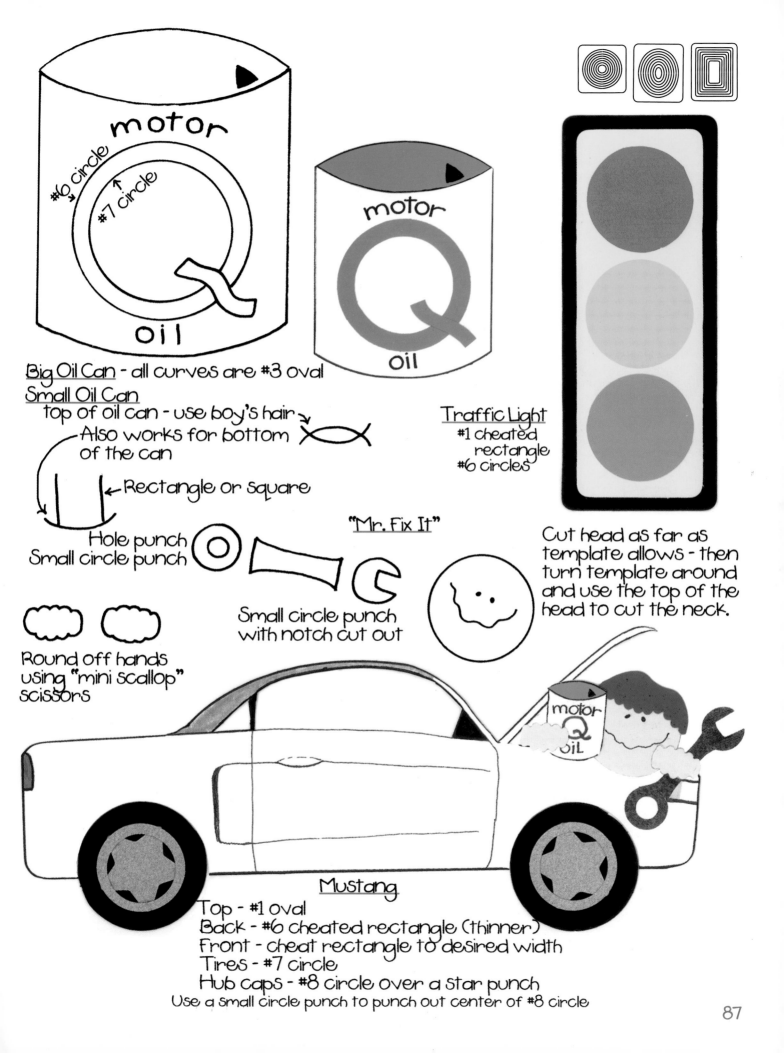

motor
#6 circle
#7 circle
Q
motor
oil

motor
Q
oil

Big Oil Can - all curves are #3 oval

Small Oil Can
  top of oil can - use boy's hair
     Also works for bottom
     of the can
        ← Rectangle or square

Hole punch
Small circle punch

Round off hands
using "mini scallop"
scissors

"Mr. Fix It"

Small circle punch
with notch cut out

Traffic Light
#1 cheated
  rectangle
#6 circles

Cut head as far as
template allows - then
turn template around
and use the top of the
head to cut the neck.

Mustang
Top - #1 oval
Back - #6 cheated rectangle (thinner)
Front - cheat rectangle to desired width
Tires - #7 circle
Hub caps - #8 circle over a star punch
Use a small circle punch to punch out center of #8 circle

head

Rectangle
punch

#6 oval

cheat
arm shorter
and thinner

Girl's
bunting ✂

Boy's
snowsuit ✂

Trim
on
hood

Bonnet

Hood ✂

Bonnet
trim

To burnish the
edge where
you've trimmed
the web, use
a fingernail
buffer for
a super
smooth finish!

Blessing
or
Christening
dress ✂

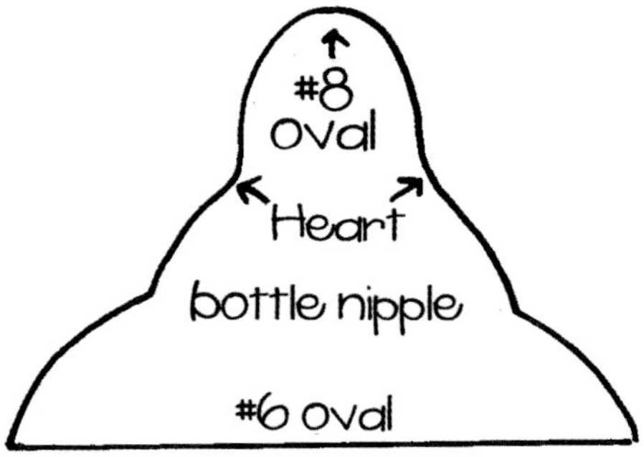

#8
oval

Heart
bottle nipple

#6 oval

bottle ring
#5 scooted square

Baby Bottle

bottle and milk
#5 rectangle

hexagon

When cutting some of the more difficult designs (ie.. the stained glass window, diaper and paper dolls), it may be helpful to trace the pattern first, then use the templates to make the cuts.

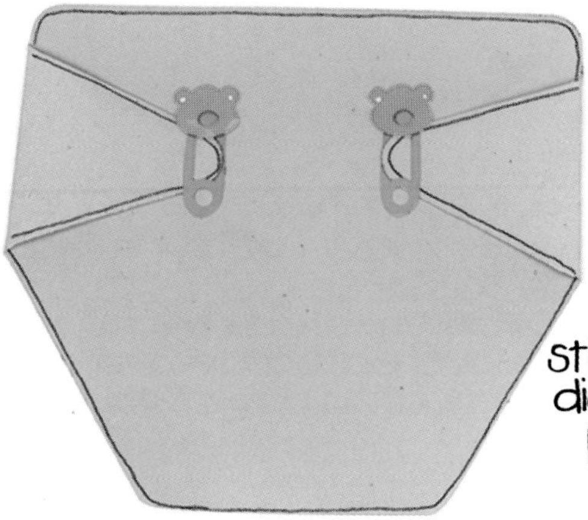

sticker
diaper
pins

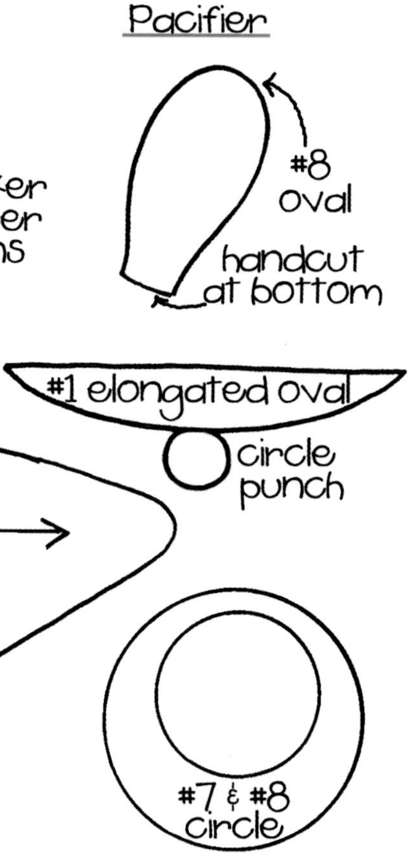

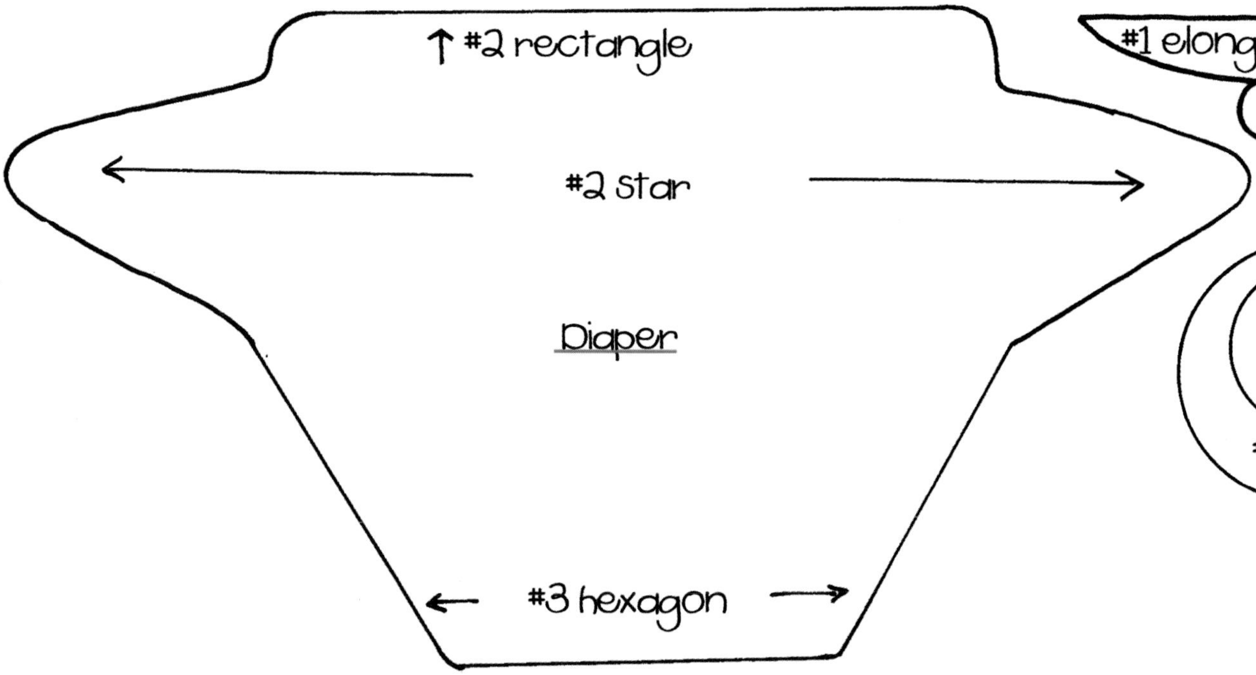

Pacifier

#8
oval

handcut
at bottom

↑ #2 rectangle

#1 elongated oval

circle
punch

← #2 star →

Diaper

#7 & #8
circle

← #3 hexagon →

89

Oval Basket

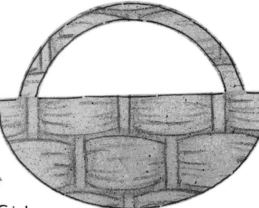

base - #4 oval
handle - #4 & #5 circle

When making baggier doll clothing it helps to slide the template to the left and right to cut each side a little bigger.

Easter Bunny Girl

bunny suit - place doll on white cardstock and trace 1/4" to 1/2" larger. Now cut along trace line with decorative scissors.
ears - cut two #7 ovals, cheated inward
inside of ears - #8 oval, cheated inward
headband - doll head cheated downward

Hexagon Basket

Cut #1 hexagon. Cut top 1/2 of #2 hexagon inside of the #1 hexagon. Fold the cut section under base.
eggs - #6 oval
bow - #6 heart
bow center - #8 hexagon

cut #1

My Big Day

#1 elongated oval

cut #3

cut #4

cut by hand

cut #2

top and bottom - #1 heart

cut #5

cut #6

NO BOYS ALLOWED

any rectangle

any cheated square or rectangle

GO TEAM

#1 pivoted heart

web on outside edge of #1 elongated oval falls here

flip template over for cuts 3 & 4 and begin with side web here

3rd cut

1st cut

Let it Snow

2nd cut

4th cut

#1 elongated oval

#1 rectangle

web of #7 rectangle used here

Happy Anniversary

any corners used here

1/2 #7 rectangle

91

OH HAPPY DAY

"Kids" Alphabet
and Alphabitties
#6 & #7 hexagon

#6 & #7
heart

just FOR YOU

#8 oval

#8 circle

#6 square

#6 cheated
rectangle

#7 cheated
rectangle

Presents
"Kids" Alphabet
and Alphabitties

SWEETIE PIE

Sweetie Pie
"Fat Dot" Alphabitties
"Big Cut" scissors
    filling - #7 hearts
    pie dish - #1 elongated oval
    crust - #1 elongated oval
        trimmed

wheels - #7 cheated
    rectangle
bumper - #1 & #4
    rectangle
plate - #7 cheated
    rectangle
cans - #7 oval &
    any square
"Fat Dot"
    Alphabitties

#8 square
    "Kids"
    Alphabitties

egg - #6 oval
shell - #6 circle
    lengthened
"Kids" Alphabitties

#7 & #8 square
    "Scrapbook"
    Alphabitties

93

We're jammin'

Log Jam
"Scrapbook" Alphabitties and "Scrapbook" Alphabet Template

round end of logs with #7 circle

logs – #1 & #3 rectangle

Wet and Wild

Drips – half of #2, #3 & #4 heart
"Funky" Alphabet Stickers

Witch
head – #6 circle
hat – #2 star
brim – square

Frankenstein
#6 square

BOO Blocks
#6 & #7 squares

Mummy
head – #6 circle
body – #5 circle

all hands – #8 circle cut in half. Trim with "scallop decorative scissors

B O O

#8 square
cheated ↑ rectangle

Snowmen
scarves

#1 circle
#2 circle

SNOWMEN

94

#4 star
"Fat Dot"
Alphabet Stickers

#8 square
#7 oval
"Fat Dot"
Alphabet
Stickers
shade squares
with gray chalk

petals & centers -
   #8 circle
leaves -
   #8 cheated circle
"kids" Alphabitties

shade with pink
and green chalk

Framing and Matting Photos

TV instructions
see page 14

The Coluzzle® nested templates were originally designed to cut photos and perfect 1/4" mats... and they do! Now lets expand on that idea and see where our creativity leads us!

The Boys

Frame your picture with the red channel (#5) Press firmly on template, cut the blue channel (#4). Now cut the green channel (#3). Discard middle frame.

#4 rectangle
(cut the inside picture first
then cut #5 and #6 rectangles)

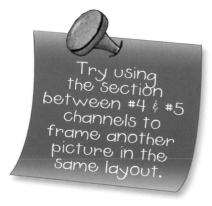

Try using the section between #4 & #5 channels to frame another picture in the same layout.

To center two openings in one mat, draw a pencil line down the center of the backside of paper. Line up channels using pencil line and edge of frame.

#1 rectangle mat
#1 cheated rectangle frame
inner mat - #3 oval

#1 rectangle
center the #2 elongated oval

corner punch

98

Helmet - #1 circle

Logo - #8 heart
Circle punch
Brim - #1 oval
Frame & picture - #1 cheated rectangle

Recreate a frame out of the elements in your photo!

#3 star
#2 star
#4 circle

Star Pupil

* Red star and rectangle are cut as one piece.

Frame - #1 & #2 rectangle
Star - #1 & #2 star

99

strips - cut a strip with the
  #1 and #2 rectangle and trim
  to desired length.
photo - #3 rectangle
mat - #1 rectangle

#2 rectangle   #1 cheated rectangle
                 #1 rectangle
              photo - #2 rectangle

Dark Blue - #1 cheated out rectangle
Light Blue - #1 rectangle

cut various sizes of ovals
or circles out of a #3 oval
(see page 9)

green frame - #1 rectangle
red frame - #3 cheated rectangle

I Believe...

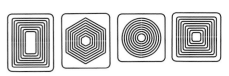

#1, #2, #3, and
#4 hexagon

Frame - #1 square
Inside - #3 & #4 circle
Daisy punch

Dallas, Sasha
and Trapper
1994

Frame _ #2 cheated rectangle
Inside - #3 rectangle

Outside frame - #1 square
Center frame - #2 square
inside frame - #3 square

Football picture - & frame
#1 cheated oval
Trim - #1 oval

#1 cheated oval

#2 cheated oval
#4 cheated circle

Dallas

State Quarterfinal Football Game Dec. 4, 1999

outside - #2 oval
inside - #4 oval

#1 cheated circle

picture - #3 oval
outside frame - #1 oval
(#1 oval trimmed with decorative
  scissors and teeny hole punched)

frames - #1 ovals
picture - #2 oval

frame - #1 rectangle
photo - #2 rectangle
basketballs - #8 circle

outside edge
is the oval puzzle
template

hand cut
to attach

#3 hearts

AVP
Best Defensive Player

volleyballs - #8 circle

On larger
pictures (i.e.,
5 x 7, 8 x 10) we
often use the
outside channel
on straight puzzle
template to trim
photos and mats.

1997

frame - #1 rectangle
photo - #2 rectangle
volleyballs - #6 & #8 circles

Puzzle Template Ideas

♫ I left my ♫ ♪
♪ ♪ ♪ heart

In
♪ San Francisco ♫

WILD

THINGS

A Day at the Zoo

Tilting the entire puzzle gives a different dimension. Notice that the photos, (above) are cut vertically but the template is tipped.

Bless the Blooms

Beach Babes At Mustang Beach

Try using any puzzle template to make a puzzle out of your child's artwork.

BIG Brothers: are the BEARY Best

Carson and Riley take care of Bailey and teach her right from wrong. June 1999

Try cutting only along the outside of the shape for a large cuddly teddy bear (this also works very well to crop those larger professional photographs).

GO FOR THE GOLD!!

A fun option with puzzles is to use paper only for a "patchwork" look. Also try using a combination of paper and photos in a collage.

Practically Perfect
TEA

Supercalifragilisticexpialidocious
Even though the sound of it
Is something quite atrocious
If you say it loud enough
You'll always sound precocious
Supercalifragilisticexpialidocious

Sept. 26, 1998